IT WAS THE WAR
OF THE TRENCHES

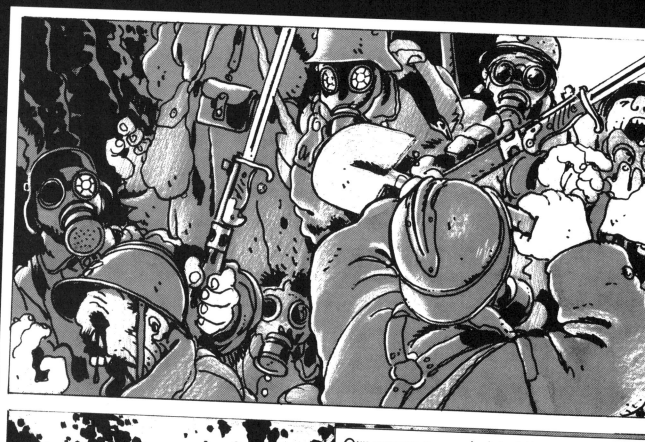

Our cannons responded, but they were poorly a[...]
our lines. We quit fooling around, we were forced[...]
could, to scramble from the trench to seek "ref[...]

d were hitting
ff as best we
een the lines.

# IT WAS THE WAR OF THE TRENCHES

Art & story by

## Jacques TARDI

*"For my grandfather."*

**FANTAGRAPHICS BOOKS**

Previously published by Fantagraphics Books:

# WEST COAST BLUES (LE PETIT BLEU DE LA CÔTE OUEST)
By Jacques Tardi and Jean-Patrick Manchette

# YOU ARE THERE (ICI MÊME)
By Jacques Tardi and Jean-Claude Forest

Edited and translated by **Kim Thompson** | Design by **Adam Grano** | Production by **Paul Baresh** | Lettering and editorial assistance by **Ian Burns, Brittany Kusa** and **Gavin Lees** | Font designed by **Allan Haverholm,** provided by **Christopher Ouzman** of **Faraos Cigarer** | Hand calligraphy by **Gavin Lees** | German dialogues by **Christa Berthommier** | Special editorial thanks to **Art Spiegelman, Françoise Mouly, Paul Karasik, Kristy Valenti** and **Gary Groth** | Associate Publisher **Eric Reynolds** | Published by **Gary Groth** and **Kim Thompson** | *It Was the War of the Trenches* (*C'Etait la guerre des tranchées*) © 1993 **Editions Casterman** | This edition © 2010 **Fantagraphics Books** | All rights reserved, permission to quote or reproduce material for reviews or notices must be obtained from **Fantagraphics Books**, in writing, at **7563 Lake City Way NE, Seattle, WA 98115** | Visit the Fantagraphics website at **www.fantagraphics** | Distributed to bookstores in the U.S. by **W.W. Norton and Company, Inc. (212-354-5500)** | Distributed to comics shops in the U.S. by **DIAMOND COMIC DISTRIBUTORS (800-452-6642)** | Distributed in Canada by **Canadian Manda Group (416-516-0911)** | First edition **February, 2010** | Printed in **Singapore** | ISBN: **978-1-60699-353-8**

# FOREWORD

*It Was the War of the Trenches* is not the work of an "historian"... This is not the history of the first World War told in comics form, but a non-chronological sequence of situations, lived by men who have been jerked around and dragged through the mud, clearly unhappy to find themselves in this place, whose only wish is to stay alive for just one more hour, whose overarching desire is to return home... in one word, for the war to be over! There are no "heroes," there is no "protagonist" in this awful collective "adventure" that is war. Nothing but a gigantic, anonymous scream of agony.

I purposefully stayed on the French side, for reasons that should be obvious. How exactly did the English react? What might the Italians have been thinking? It's hard enough to get inside the head of a young man in the year 1914. Of course, most of the nations involved in the conflict are mentioned, there is a constant stream of references to the Germans, the "Boches" (I used this term without malice because it was accurate to the period). I hope to have been sufficiently clear that no one will accuse me of score-settling, let alone nationalism, and I did want to mention the unfortunate citizens of our "colonies" who were cheerfully invited to join in the "party." What retained my attention is the man—whatever his color or his nationality —who is considered disposable, whose life is worth nothing in his master's hands... a banal observation that remains valid to this day.

I was frequently moved as I gazed upon the photographs furnished by my invaluable archivist, Jean-Pierre Verney... images of poor souls, German or French, all of them displaying the hundred-yard stare, because regardless of the pose, their anxiety and fear shine through. I never ceased to wonder: How was anyone able to stand his ground under fire? How was anyone able to sleep? To wake up? From what source could one draw a modicum of hope to provide energy? The rain, the mud, the depression, the cold, the shells... Self-inflicted wounds, mutinies, desertion, now those I understand...

I haven't told the "whole story" because that would be a monstrous enterprise. From when I first heard my grandfather's stories, I've always been haunted by the desire to try to create an account of this early part of the 20th century. I consulted books, which I list in the bibliography and which often inspired me; I used them as departure points for episodes which I then fictionalized. It was not my goal to create a catalog of weapons and uniforms—although I did, of course, use documentation —even less so to render an accounting: How many shells per square meter, the number of men involved in such-and-such offensive. I avoided any and all "historical" events that have long ago been analyzed and filed away by historians, or better yet, related by witnesses; it is from the latter that I preferred to draw certain information. Because it should be noted that the "official" numbers vary widely from one historical work to another. I wasn't there, so I had to rely on stories that were debatable to varying degrees, some of them questionable or contradictory. Here too the "specialist" will have his five cents to put in.

The only thing that interests me is man and his suffering, and it fills me with rage. This is our history, Europe's history, and the 20th century's—the century of industrialization and death, born in Sarajevo. The "First World War," an innovation that seems to have been embraced: Gas broadened our horizons, gave us new ideas, it was all quite "modern." These ideas were already inherent in Cro-Magnon man: Man carries this brutality within. Only the methods of extermination become more sophisticated, and in this context, we can salute the war of 1914-1918! Europe... 1917, the Russian revolution and the arrival of the Americans... we've been living with the consequences of these events for decades. Since then the situation has changed, I nearly wrote "evolved"... Every November 11th some ancient veteran is given a medal (how many of them are left at this point?). He was 20 years old in 1915 and his youth and his future were stolen from him. So... please don't make fun of him...

**TARDI (1994)**

## SPECIAL THANKS

*Now, about the soldier who's being judged in a classroom... are his hands tied?*

No, no, the verdict hasn't been handed down yet. He's standing at attention, flanked by two armed soldiers... You can draw him bareheaded or with a cap, or with his helmet under his arm, or his helmet on his head.

*He's wearing his greatcoat?*

...Or his tunic... belted, but without the cartridge belt.

*By the way, this tunic, does it have any buttons on the back? A half belt?*

No, nothing; seven buttons down the front, buttoned up in the middle, and a high collar.

*Okay, so, the tribunal...*

Well... You might have a colonel, a commander, a captain, two lieutenants. The lieutenants might have come from the front, you can draw them in their greatcoats, their helmets on the table in front of them; the others, in formal dress with their decorations. All sitting behind a long table.

*When he's being shot, is the soldier tied to a stake, blindfolded?*

Not necessarily, only the ones who request it... Sometimes they place a white piece of cardboard over his heart... There is only one blank in the firing squad.

*Twelve soldiers?*

Or eight, it depends... You could have the officer addressing the soldiers, saying, "Don't shoot over his head, or we'll have to do it all over again!"

*Uh, no, I can't fit that in... Too bad, that's a bit I could use, I'll revisit it at a later date.*

All of this over the telephone... I'm speaking with Jean-Pierre Verney, he knows everything about 1914-1918, down to the smallest detail. I use his services on a daily basis. Each and every panel of this book required one or more long telephone conversations. I've lost count of how many documents and objects he put at my disposal, I thank him for his expertise, his congeniality, and his patience in helping me. **TARDI**

October 1917...

The three blows have been struck... just like in the theatre... but the first came courtesy of a 15-pound mortar shell, the second of a 105-mm cannon discharging a 35-pound projectile, and the third, a 400-mm one. Weight of the resulting missile: 2,000 pounds!

The day begins with the artillery shooting off ton after ton of explosives. The muzzles of the cannons turn red hot and their servants go deaf.

They are discharging weapons manufactured in the Ruhr by Krupp Enterprises, in Germany...

...and the retort comes courtesy of arms manufactured in France by Schneider, by the *Le Creusots* enterprises, as well as the St. Etiennes, the St. Chamonds, and other great families...

The calibers of these mechanical marvels grow larger and larger, the projectiles increasingly powerful. The enormous cannons set on rails are capable of sowing death as far as 10 miles away!

Ingenuity without end... it's an ongoing race, on both sides, to gain the upper hand in terms of firepower, and to benefit industry, thriving as it does in this time of war.

Men are being shot at... nothing new there, as the war of the trenches has already been going on for three years...

...what's most astonishing is that there remains any life whatsoever within these holes, given how many shells are launched every day onto such a small area.

These men have dug trenches, built shelters in the earth, and learned how to live in the mud like rats. Here we see the French.

On the other side, it's more or less the same: But the trenches are better organized, because they're German. The French say *"les boches"* when they speak of their enemies, out of contempt, out of hatred, or maybe out of stupidity because where war is concerned it always comes down to stupidity.

On either side, neither Germans nor Frenchmen have any real reason to kill one another even though, when it all began, they'd set off with a similar impulse toward war. Today they would like nothing more than to go home and are sorry that they ever obeyed their commanders... but their respective commanders have no desire to continue the slaughter on their own...

...which would make things considerably simpler, would be far less expensive, and would spare thousands of lives — because the slaves far outnumber the commanders — and so nothing ever changes, for men are mere sheep and the slaughterhouse is where they have been told to stay...

The point of contact between the two armies has stabilized; this is the front. Between the front lines there is an area everyone calls "No Man's Land"... for there are Britons in this war, too.

On a fairly regular basis, the soldiers are forced to emerge from the trenches and horrific hand-to-hand combat erupts in the No Man's Land. This is how the game is played: The French try to overrun the Germans' front line, and the Germans try to overrun the front lines of the French.

In the No Man's Land the following are to be found: barbed wire, placed there to fend off surprise attacks; dead men from the previous night's offensives; the dying wounded; and all manner of debris, as well as shell-holes filled with rainwater.

The place is hopping at night. Men are sent to observe the doings on the other side; to perform upkeep on the network of barbed wire; and to hit the enemy with the goal of bringing back prisoners, recovering wounded men, or burying dead men who are too visible and too much of a drain on morale, like a buddy's corpse hanging, rotting, from the barbed wire.

In this image, in the foreground, you can see a dead soldier: Private BINET.

BINET was manning the parapet when the Captain — who did not put his feet on the front line very often — himself gave FAUCHEUX the order to go on reconnaissance in the shell-hole next to the ruins, where we had an advance post from which no news had been forthcoming.

The Captain gave FAUCHEUX another slew of directives, and he left around noon, lugging his satchel filled with grenades. Before going over the edge of the trench, he handed BINET a little booklet bound in blue paper, the kind children use to protect their schoolbooks.

BINET watched for a long time as FAUCHEUX crept through the No Man's Land and then he lost sight of him. Had he arrived safely at the ruins of the farmhouse, near the shell-hole? That afternoon we heard a grenade go off. Then nothing...

5.

BINET spent the rest of the day and all night peering through the slit, watching for FAUCHEUX'S return. Although he was relieved of sentry duty, he couldn't stop anxiously scrutinizing the devastated terrain. He did not return to his dug-out to get some sleep. A baleful dawn broke over the war and the mud. FAUCHEUX seemed to have been swallowed up by a night that refused to give him back.

The day wore on without incident. Still no news from FAUCHEUX. At dusk, the battalion was relieved.

The soldiers slogged through the labyrinth of trenches and tunnels all the way to the rear line, where they were finally beyond the range of the Germans' sight and could walk in the open.

At dawn, after a six-kilometer march, they arrived in the village beyond the rear lines where they were supposed to rest for a few days. They knew they'd left the combat area behind because everyone could see the two policemen.

There were plenty of stories going around about those policemen, always harassing the soldiers, even as they themselves stayed well behind the lines. During the retreat, they had even shot laggards. Apparently some veteran soldiers had strung up some policemen in the wake of an argument. BINET wasn't opposed to the notion of hanging them... in fact, he was all for it!

Exhausted, they continued on to the barns and the sheds of the farms intended for them — the actual residential houses that were still standing being reserved for the officers, already in their beds...

With money, some men have secured more comfortable lodgings, but for most, the bedding will consist of rotting straw.

Time to rest. A few days on the far side of the village, safe relative to the trenches, and also the opportunity for a little bit of isolation, to escape the crowding that weighed so heavily on BINET. In the meantime, this barn where they'd just arrived was like a room back at the barracks. The "buddies" — the obscene jokes, the mass of bodies, the heaviness of the spirits, and especially... the smells.

There were the nice guys, always trying to be helpful; resourceful put-on artists; kiss-asses; morons whose stupidity was almost touching; men brimming with goodwill, lifelong idiots...

As everywhere else, there was the intolerable pain in the ass; the know-it-all;, the Parisian; and, perhaps worst of all, the instructor intoning his lesson, believing himself to still be in his classroom, the pedagogue lording if over the others.

There were also quiet ones, the kind BINET preferred. There were times when it became almost unbearable, and BINET loathed them all as one... He was sorely lacking in team spirit.

There had been no picking and choosing... They were all being sent to their death, that was EGALITE. LIBERTE, now, that would've been if he'd been allowed to go home... He was thinking about home, BINET was.

He lived alone on the 5th floor, the little window in the A of DUFAYEL.

On the ground floor lived FLOCARD the butcher, and his least favorite thing in the world was neighborhood-store chit-chat...

On the second floor, the BRIGNONS, who would stink up the staircase all year long with their cabbages and with the farts produced by the consumption of said vegetable.

On the third, the MAGNINS and their awful, obnoxious kids.

On the fourth, the widow SARCELLE, always spying on everybody else, a dreadful gossip... the kind that sets off wars.

On the sixth, Miss BROZILLE, a spinster who liked to rise early. Constantly pacing in her two-room apartment, her steps resounded in his head like a deep-sea diver's boots... no possibility of communication, Miss BROZILLE was alone in her world... BINET would have taken great satisfaction in killing her.

The maid's chambers at the top housed a whole cluster of fallen humanity, filthy and destitute.

He also loathed the residents of his building, BINET did... As far as he was concerned, cities were composed of similar buildings, and FRANCE was made up of cities; of course there was also the rural population, about which the less said, the better! That was his country. THAT was what BINET was being forced to fight for... for those people!!! He would've been in the trenches on the other side, if he'd been born slightly more to the East... it was a matter of pure chance that he happened to belong to this particular nation.

There was really no reason whatsoever to die for any country, no matter which one!... That was how BINET felt about it.

...People were quarreling around the mobile soup kitchen... morons... that was the French all over!

Peace and quiet... that was to be found among the dead. As far as the side he was obliged to defend, BINET had learned as early as the schoolyard during recess what real cruelty was... So much for FRATERNITÉ, your brotherhood.

To be sure, people were no better on one side than the other, all they wanted was to cut their neighbor's throat... that it turned into war was to be expected. In his satchel, he came across FAU-CHEUX's little booklet. There were addresses, notes, a photograph. He was surely dead, FAUCHEUX, and his booklet was a bother to BINET.

Mister... How many Krauts've you killed?

10.

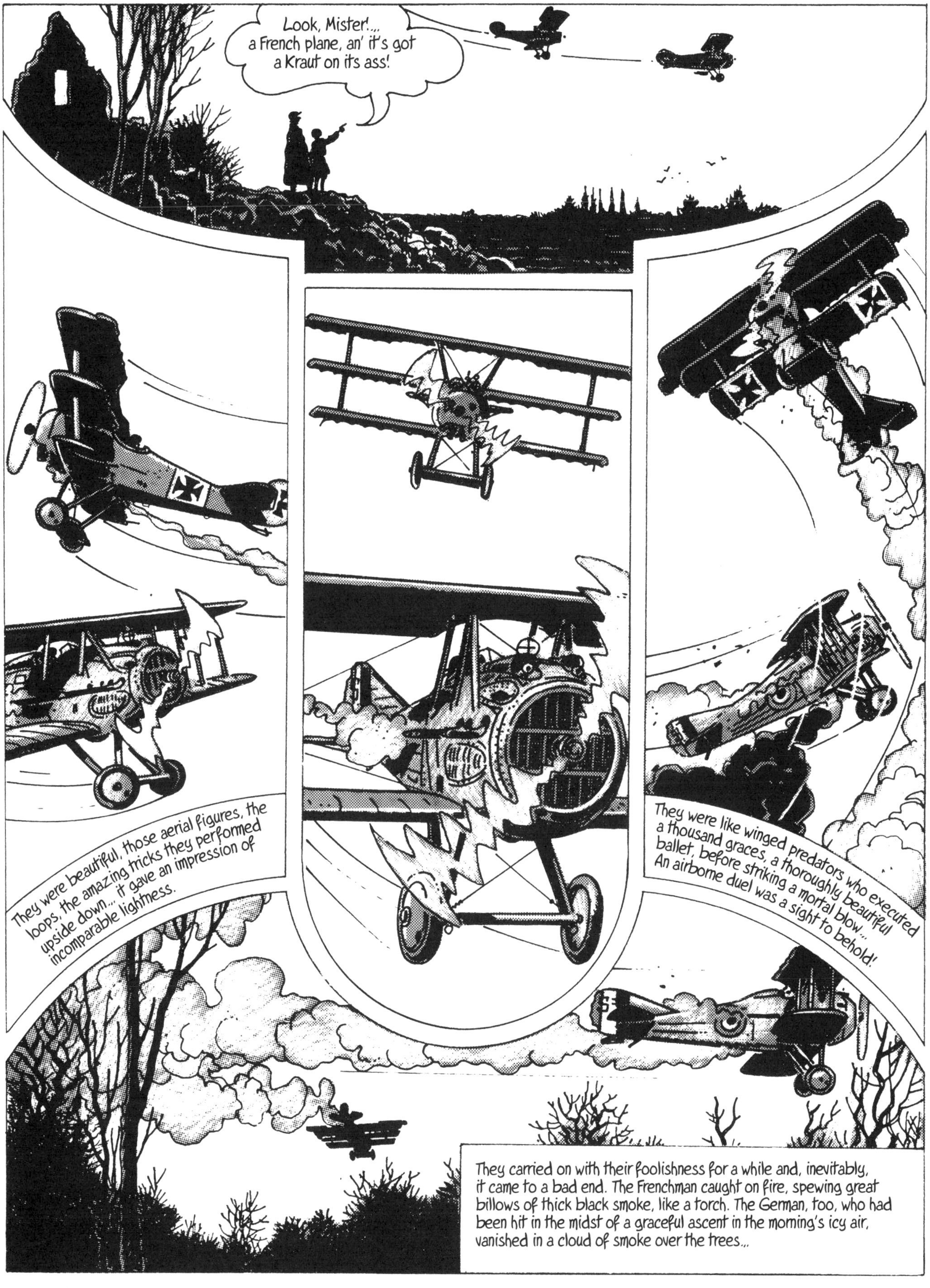
Look, Mister!...
a French plane, an' it's got
a Kraut on its ass!
They were beautiful, those aerial figures, the loops, the amazing tricks they performed upside down... it gave an impression of incomparable lightness.
They were like winged predators who executed a thousand graces, a thoroughly beautiful ballet, before striking a mortal blow...
An airborne duel was a sight to behold!
They carried on with their foolishness for a while and, inevitably, it came to a bad end. The Frenchman caught on fire, spewing great billows of thick black smoke, like a torch. The German, too, who had been hit in the midst of a graceful ascent in the morning's icy air, vanished in a cloud of smoke over the trees...

There was nothing left to look at on the road, so BINET and the kid headed back to the village. It was better down here, although God knows one felt heavy with one's boots deep in the mud.

How much does a plane cost?

Look here, kid, war ain't no vacation, you'd be better off at school.

Odd things were happening in the schools by the front. There were strange teachers who weren't teaching the history of France, but making it. Not that we could do anything about it... They were our superiors.

LUCIANA was from Corsica, he spoke no French. He hadn't understood the order he'd been given during an offensive. He hadn't executed it. He had "disobeyed."

He was judged in a heartbeat. ABANDONING YOUR POST ON THE BATTLEFIELD! He didn't understand the sentence. He was executed. They made the newcomers to the front do it.

Soldiers weren't just taking a break on the rear lines, they were being put through exercises and maneuvers so that they might return even more war-hungry to the front line, which is what the regiment did after 15 days spent in the village.

It was back to life in the trenches, in the same, relatively quiet, sector. Every day the Germans would launch a five-minute burst of artillery fire, around suppertime. The French would respond immediately. The men would stay in the shelters. These barrages were not particularly lethal; you could almost set your watch by them.

As for the rest of it, it was same old story: reinforce the networks of barbed wire, build up the damaged shelters, dig fresh latrines, or watch at the slits, eyes fixed on the No Man's Land, one's mind back at home.

The ruins by the artillery hole hadn't changed. Only the wreckage of the German plane freshened up the scenery a bit. BINET figured it might be the aeroplane he'd seen go down in flames, on the rear lines with the kid. There had been no word from FAUCHEUX.

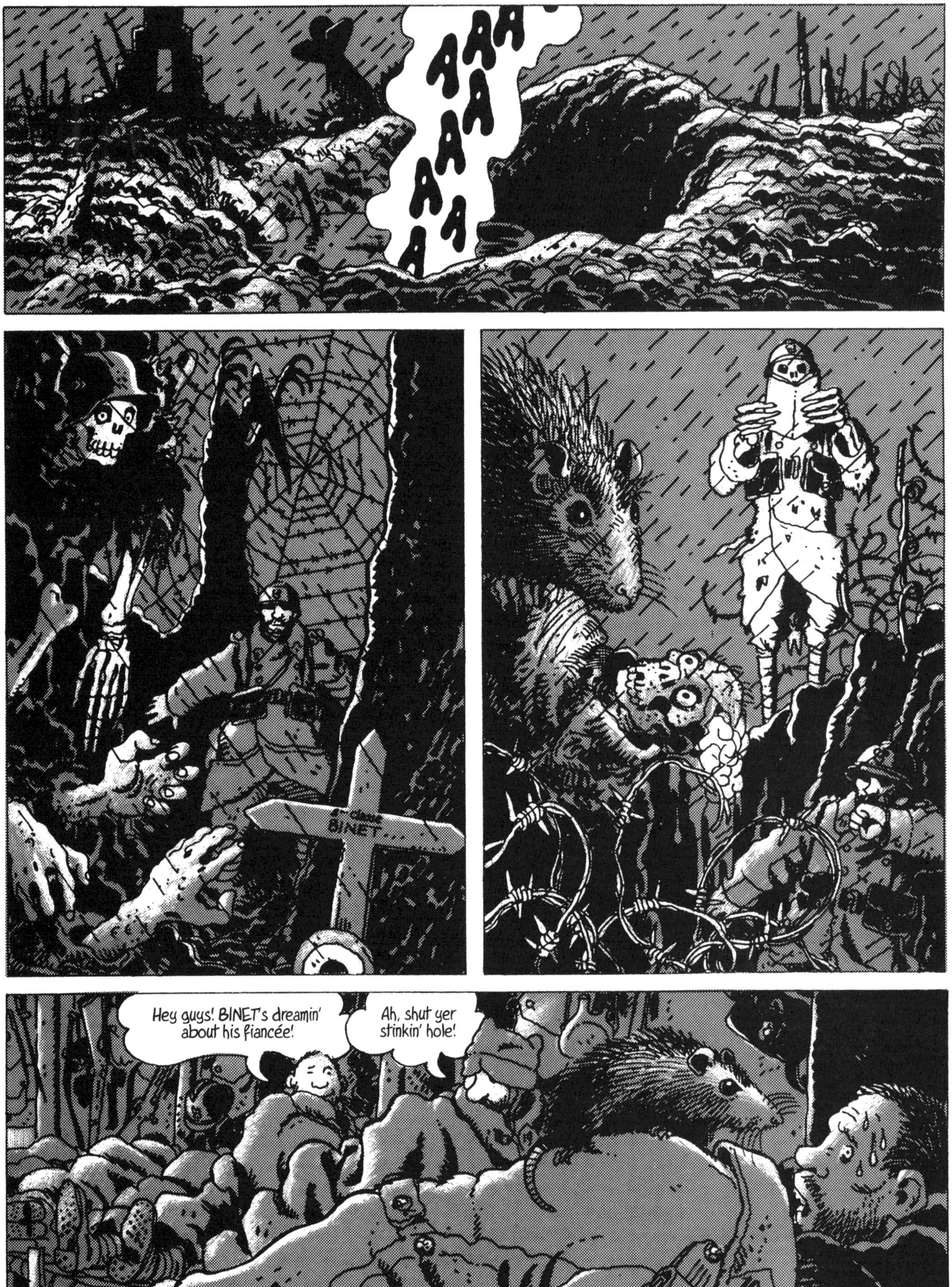
AAAAAAAAA
BINET
Hey guys! BINET's dreamin' about his fiancée!
Ah, shut yer stinkin' hole!

BINET crawled out of the shelter. FAUCHEUX? He'd never returned from his recon mission by the shell-hole. He was dead for sure! But it kept BINET from sleeping.

CHARROI was on watch, at the parapet.

BINET! What the fuck're you doin' here?

Can't get any shuteye... if y'want, I'll take over your watch.

No shit? Even with the rain an' all? Suit y'self!

He had a point, the rain wasn't exactly contributing to the charm of this frigid October night spent outdoors and during wartime...

Delighted, CHARROI had headed back into the shelter... And BINET had stayed, but not to count the raindrops, let alone stand guard. He clambered over the edge of the trench...

...and began to run, hunched over, across the No Man's Land!!!

15.

BINET was running toward the shell-hole where FAUCHEUX had to be hiding... There had been rumors about that outpost in the ruins, right smack in the middle, between the frontlines... controlled sometimes by one side, sometimes by the other... they'd stopped any serious fighting over it... which had worked out for everyone...

There'd been stories of fraternization... People trading sausages for tobacco while waiting for things to blow over... at least that was something... keep just a small part of the world set aside from the war...

FAUCHEUX had probably set up some little business along those lines. The Captain who'd sent him out there was probably in on the scheme. Obviously some ultrasecret deal struck with the Krauts.

...he'd been wounded, FAUCHEUX had, and been back on the front line just for a short while... sneaking out cocaine from the hospitals, and consuming it in spoons on the front lines... The Krauts probably wouldn't have minded a taste either... That was everything that was running through BINET's mind, pell-mell...

...not that he gave a shit! It was curiosity, mostly, that had prompted him to crawl out of his hole... FAUCHEUX had to be hiding... unless he was dead, unless someone had balked at playing the game... some guy who wasn't in the loop, who'd queered the whole deal. Then again, BINET might simply have gone mad... there was that possibility, too.

The machine gun was concealed just a few yards away, within the ruins... The burst was short. BINET took five in the belly. The bullets penetrated his flesh without difficulty, perforating his intestines and his left lung, causing irreparable damage. He felt a sort of tearing sensation, a pain difficult to describe. Words were too weak. His suffering went beyond suffering, so that he almost felt no pain... but he knew it was all over for him now.

At 4:25 a.m. he fell to his knees, his legs no longer able to support him. All the blood was draining from his body, filling up his tunic... It was an unpleasant feeling. His blood was warm, turned cold immediately by the ambient air... a ghastly wind was blowing over the battlefield, and BINET couldn't keep from thinking about the day that was just dawning... Would he survive the night? Would he see it break, this day?... Was it worth it to stay alive for it? He pondered this, and then he realized that the time for pondering was over.

His apartment building flashed in front of his eyes...

He saw the widow SARCELLE, the BRIGNONS, the FLOCARDS, the MAGNINS and their rotten kids, the BROZILLE woman... they were all there... they all seemed happy.

As for me, I took a good look around, as I'd been told... and I saw: The ruins, the German with his machine gun, the shell-hole with FAUCHEUX at the bottom of it, the downed Fokker, and BINET who'd just checked out from the whole deal... I was in the front row... like in the theatre... There was gas, too... So I headed home.

BINET saw a soldier as the day broke... He noticed his gas mask, and also that it was no longer raining... He got a chuckle out of that mask... He couldn't smell the gas... He was already dead.

When I returned I filed my report on what I'd seen, exactly as the Captain had ordered me to... The Captain said "Fine...," looking annoyed, and he left.

We got a new Captain. I don't really know what happened back at HQ, but three days later, the artillery — ours, that is — pounded the hell out of the ruins. There was nothing left of that advance post... It was too much trouble... The location was just plain lousy...

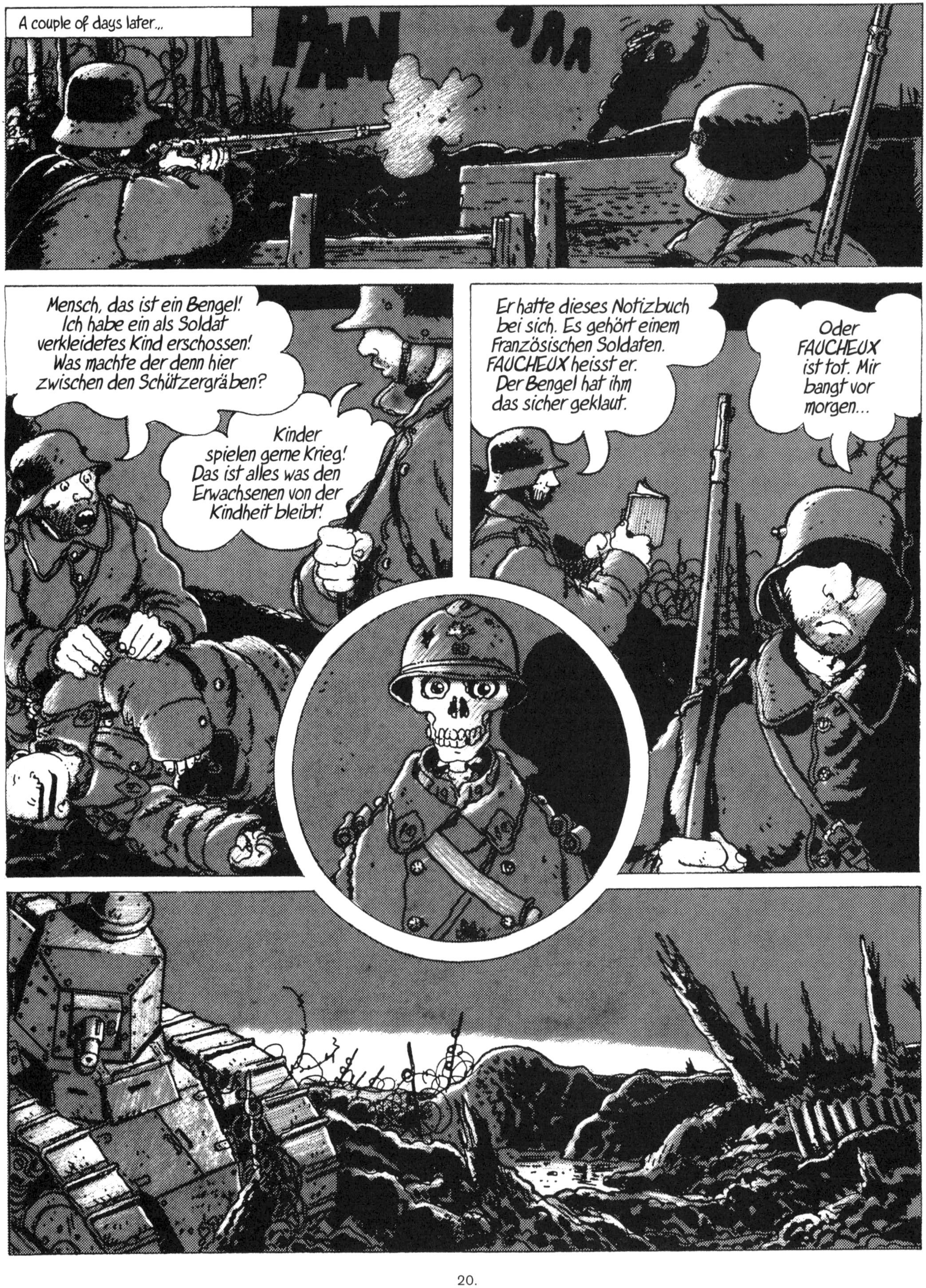
A couple of days later...
PAN
AAA
Mensch, das ist ein Bengel! Ich habe ein als Soldat verkleidetes Kind erschossen! Was machte der denn hier zwischen den Schützergräben?
Kinder spielen gerne Krieg! Das ist alles was den Erwachsenen von der Kindheit bleibt!
Er hatte dieses Notizbuch bei sich. Es gehört einem Französischen Soldaten. FAUCHEUX heisst er. Der Bengel hat ihm das sicher geklaut.
Oder FAUCHEUX ist tot. Mir bangt vor morgen...

The soldier slogs heavily through the mud... He's loaded down, lugging two full jugs—soup, still hot—flagons of wine, bread slung across his back like a rifle, and haversacks full of grub. He's searching for the entrance to the tunnel that will lead him to the trench where the other fellows are waiting for their dinner. He's pretty much out in the open and that's all he can think about right now. The occasional stray bullet ends its flight right at the level of his leggings—it plunges into the yellow muck, still potentially lethal. The soldier's boots get stuck in the mud. It's still night. The only light is a glow on the horizon with, from time to time, some sort of lightning or a series of brighter lights, and a low rumble, an incessant buzzing noise that starts churning up your guts if you don't put it out of your mind. Most of the shit is happening up north—back here things are quiet, or so they say. From time to time, a routine gunshot, to which our gunners respond half-heartedly. It's the bored Boche, in want of targets, who may be the most dangerous... All of this is running through this soldier's mind, he can't wait to find his tunnel again so as to be out of harm's way... And the soup is cooling! He thinks about the cold, too, and his sopping-wet feet, about the roughness of the collar on his overcoat...

With every step, his ill-fitting helmet knocks against his right ear, which is frozen solid, ready to shatter like glass. Fucking crummy gear! Truly, no respect for the taxpayer who is fighting for his country! Here his thoughts stop. A flare has just been shot off and is serenely drifting down, suspended from its parachute, right above the soldier, illuminating everything, abso-lutely everything... As if being lost wasn't bad enough, now he's taken on the role of target. And right away the crackling begins! A machine gun volley. So he throws himself to the ground, on his belly. He takes a mean blow to the kidneys from the butt of his Lebel rifle. The soup spills out onto the ground, he can feel the warmth of the broth on his thigh. He tries to extricate his rifle and gets tangled up in the straps of his haversack, his fin-gers caked in mud. Confusion, chaos, panic, and he can't move! There's a lot of shooting—close by, too. Two minutes ago it was quiet as the grave, it's like night and day. Bullet hits, inches from his body. For sure he's going to end up taking one, right there, like an idiot, lying in the mud... lying in shit, as a matter of fact... Jesus, the stench! At least one Boche must be rotting away nearby. You stop noticing the corpses, there are so many, layers of them, French ones, German ones, you step all over them, one stops covering them up... You live with them and find uses for them, you can hang your canteen on a foot jutting out above the trench... This particular stiff, he's really stinking up the joint, though... but that's the least of it... Anyway, there's a hell of a lot of shooting going on and he can't move, but he's got to... He stays put for at least an hour, it's hard to judge time in those moments when one's body is rigid with terror. The only place showing any movement at all is up and down his spine, against his skin... a highway of lice. They've also become part of the norm, the lice have, along with the rats and the runs. The "75" cannon joins the chorus, it's in the game for the duration, through the rest of the night, maybe tomorrow

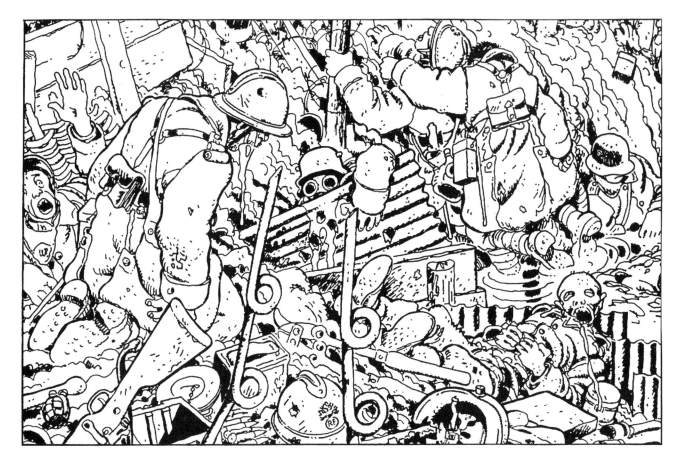

as well. A shell falls a short distance away and here comes the shrapnel, clumps of ground carved out from deep down, and mud, too. The soldier, his two hands clenched over his helmet, tries to shield his neck. It's a ridiculous gesture, considering all the crap that's raining down on him, all those pieces of iron that are being driven into the ground and that would like nothing better than to drill into his fragile flesh... even his helmet will be useless to stop them. The shooting heats up. He's got to bug out. Where is that fucking tunnel, the trench, shelter?

Sunrise. Everyone's warrior ardor has cooled, and silence falls. As the darkness recedes the soldier realizes he's spent the night lying on top of a corpse, his two hands buried in its guts. What he thought was mud was in fact loathsome, rotting flesh. As hardened as one is, as used to the horror, indifferent to steaming entrails pouring out of split-open bodies, this is not a pleasant discovery... What about diseases? What if he had a cut on his hands?... Tetanus, gangrene, who knows what... His first thought: Find water... wash his hands in some disgusting puddle.

Proceeding hunched over, he comes across the communications tunnel. Upon his arrival, they bellyache a bit about the lost soup and the muddy bread but they'll end up eating it anyway.

The soldier spent the morning searching for water, without finding any... He wiped himself off thoroughly on the tails of his coat. This happened at Verdun. My grandmother was the one who told me this story, my grandfather's story. I was five years old, grampa had been there for the whole war, he'd emerged from it somewhat the worse for wear. While she talked, he was dozing, his book open on the wax tablecloth of the kitchen table. Had it faded from his memory? He never brought it up... But at night, I'd be plunged into his horror. The putrefied corpse, and

my grandfather with both his hands buried in its belly... On his deathbed, he pushed away the curate who'd come to give him the final rites. He told him that if God existed there wouldn't be any wars... that it was all bullshit. He'd been marked by it... truly he had. One year later, grandmother followed him into the grave.

When I read my first real book with typeset text and no more than a handful of illustrations, it told the edifying tale of a dog who followed his master into the trench, fought the war at his side, bit Germans, saved his wounded master—he was a captain, a hero who returned to his beautiful fiancée at the end (having won the war single-handedly). I've forgotten the title and the name of the author, but there are passages that come to mind even as I bring it up. That was my very first book... luck of the draw, I guess. I've read others since then, on the same subject... all kinds, from every viewpoint... From *Fire* to *Wooden Crosses*, through *All Quiet on the Western Front* and *Steel Storms*, just to name the best. But my favorite remains *Fear*, by Gabriel Chevalier, and the early chapters of *Journey to the End of the Night*. And I would always see grampa, with his canteens and his bread, sprawled across the dead man.

People ask me, "More soldier tales, Tardi? When're you coming out from your trench?..." References to veterans, berets, decorations, flags over the Arc de Triomphe, November 11th... but I'm afraid we are all of us still down here, down in the trenches... East, West... More precisely, in the no man's land, on the field... between the lines... where the actual battle takes place! In fact, in all of that, it's not so much a matter of the 1914-1918 War as of WAR... From trench mortars to neutron bombs... It's the upcoming one that worries me. **TARDI**

"The time had come for war to revive, in France, the sense of the ideal and of the divine." (Generak REBILLOT, *Libre Parole*, December 13, 1914.)

The shells gouged open the tortured earth, where thousands of men cowered in recently dug shelters. It was the war of the trenches.

The shells kept falling. They unearthed the dead, who sometimes were tossed into the tattered trees and dangled there, mockingly enacting the future of those yet living.

My name is Ernst WOHL-GEMUT. I am alone, on watch at this frontline post. Yesterday at dusk, a Frenchman crawled in my direction. I could make him out very clearly. I had all the time in the world to watch him. I had decided not to shoot if he went the other way, but he kept coming toward me. He was heading straight for my shelter. I hoped that he would turn around. He came closer still and I shot. At that point, he was only a few yards away. I killed him, without joy, only because this is war and that's the way things are.

My name is Paul Carpentier. I heard DUFOUR scream all night. Both of us had been on watch at this listening post; we had orders not to move until we were relieved. DUFOUR heard a noise coming from the other side. He crawled out to see what the hell the Hun was up to, just forty or fifty feet away. I saw him get hit in the stomach. He called for me to come and bring him back. I didn't dare move; I was afraid, and besides, I had orders to stay here. He howled all night. He cursed me, he cursed the army, he cursed his mother. I have but one hope now: that I'll get killed in turn.

DUFOUR died at dawn, of course... He was given just a short moment's respite. His suffering abated for a few seconds, he regained a taste for life, and that's when he died. Condemned men often expire at dawn, after a whole night of pointless suffering.

Then the big cannons far behind the lines started firing, in order to remind everyone that the war was still on and the time for hope was still far away; they had not yet had their fill of warm entrails, the kind that spill out of a man's belly when it's ripped open. The war was just entering its third year...

November 25, 1916...

Corporal LECERF had been sent out between the lines to inspect the network of barbed wire...

LECERF advanced warily into No Man's Land. The sector was calm that day . . .

His comrades from the platoon heard the shot and saw him go down.

LAFONT and LECERF knew each other well.,. They were friends, about the same age, both typographers in Montreuil. LAFONT squatted in the muddy trench and tried to relive the way it had all started for him.

It had been a hot and muggy day. Alarming rumors were flying around: rumors of a possible war back East; This assassination business: the murder of the Archduke, one month ago, at Sarajevo. Everything might have continued as before, but this was August 2, 1914...a Sunday.

On the street, some people had gathered at the foot of the wall. They were speaking excitedly to each other. There was a recently posted announcement on the wall. People were gesturing, calling to one another, commenting on the poster.

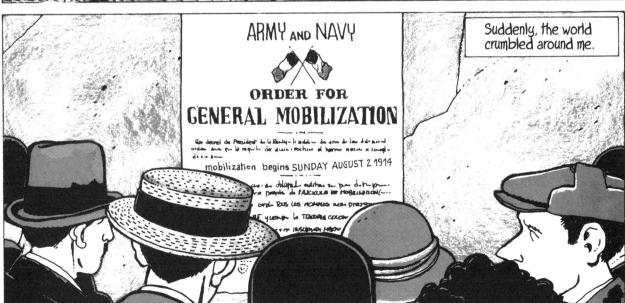

Suddenly, the world crumbled around me.

x

27.

The poster spoke of the greatest scourge man had ever created for himself: WAR. And yet the crowd was anything but distraught: made up of people who usually despised each other, it was now united in a communion of joy and hatred. Hatred for the Germans, hatred for the *Boches* they were going to crush with ease.

WAR! Within a week, twenty million men had dropped everything to go kill other men. Some of them were told: it's time for revenge, TO BERLIN! The others were told: *NACH PARIS!* And from the civil servant to the factory worker, they all left with the conviction that they were going to cover themselves with glory and enjoy a vacation. Within a week, the Germans, the Austrians, the British, the Belgians, the Russians, the Italians, the Turks, and the French had all gone off to war.

"Men are sheep. Which makes possible armies and wars. They die, victims of their own stupid docility." (Gabriel CHEVALIER, *La Peur*) ("Fear")

A band in a sidewalk café struck up *La Marseillaise*. In a common burst of patriotism, the patrons rose to their feet and intoned the national anthem. Only one man did not deign to get up. Why? Did he not share the enthusiasm of the moment? Was he the only rational person in the room? Did he recall past defeats?

They called the old man a spy bought off by the Germans, a traitor, a *Boche*.

That day, a Sunday, on the terrace of a café, I chanced to see one of the first victims of the war...

This was what was going through LAFONT's mind as he sat in an isolated corner of the trench. Since the beginning of the war, two years ago, he had been in all the battles. His regiment had been rebuilt virtually from the bottom up, because it had suffered so many casualties; its ranks now included only a handful of its original men. He was one of them, long since accustomed to the mud, the fear, and the death.

A shell exploded, not far from where he crouched, alone with his thoughts.

Private LAFONT died on November 25, 1916.

March 1917.

Some fellas, you're pleased to hear they bought it... and the one they're bringing back in pieces on that stretcher, can't say his death upsets me!

We called him "GASPARD"... He'd taken to hunting rats 'cause of the bounty: five cents a tail. He sold us rotten booze and had schemes goin' every which way.

One night when the trench flooded, one poor bastard drowned. But GASPARD made it out.

The cross served as a landmark for everyone, including artillerymen who used it to adjust their shots. So it was useful... both to the *Boches* and to us.

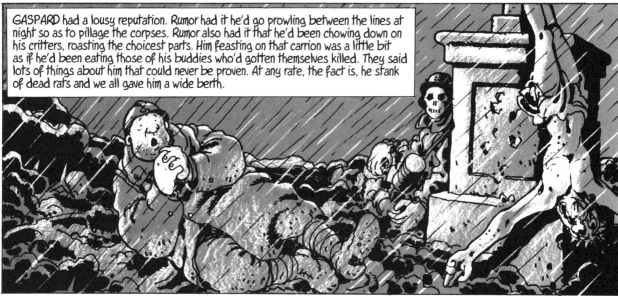

GASPARD had a lousy reputation. Rumor had it he'd go prowling between the lines at night so as to pillage the corpses. Rumor also had it that he'd been chowing down on his critters, roasting the choicest parts. Him feasting on that carrion was a little bit as if he'd been eating those of his buddies who'd gotten themselves killed. They said lots of things about him that could never be proven. At any rate, the fact is, he stank of dead rats and we all gave him a wide berth.

When he was discovered, dozens of huge rats who'd found a hiding place and shelter in his belly had scattered, reluctantly. He was all skinny and in two pieces, GASPARD was... we had a tough time recognizing him.

November 27, 1916. A bad omen: For two hours now, the French artillery has been hammering the German lines nonstop.

The 115th Infantry readies itself for an assault on the enemy trenches, despite yesterday's failed attempts. The men are exhausted. Behind them, the 20th Company is being held in reserve.

On the frontline, the 3rd Company is scheduled to charge at 4:30. At the moment, the artillery is laying down a barrage.

My name is Jean DESBOIS. I belong to the 3rd Company which is going to charge as soon as the artillery holds its fire. We'll climb over the edge of the trench and we'll be out in the open, exposed to the German machine guns. Yesterday and the day before, it turned out to be impossible for us to advance, we had to fall back to our positions and wait it out. We'd hoped we'd get sent to the rear lines for a few days' rest. Nothing doing, our officers are digging in their heels and despite our losses, we're going to charge again. I'm afraid of being killed. Yesterday I had a near miss, I've been lucky so far, but I have the feeling I'm going to die today...

4:29. The French artillery, far back behind the lines, ceases its barrage.

The soldiers, deafened by cannon fire, know what this sudden quiet means.

Then the shrill racket of the whistles... ATTACK!

"The 75 falls quiet. The captain pulls his revolver from its holster. Everyone understands. Then a moment of mortal terror... Charge! Ah! The divine moment is upon us..." (Abbé SERTILLANGES, Madeleine, May 9, 1915.)

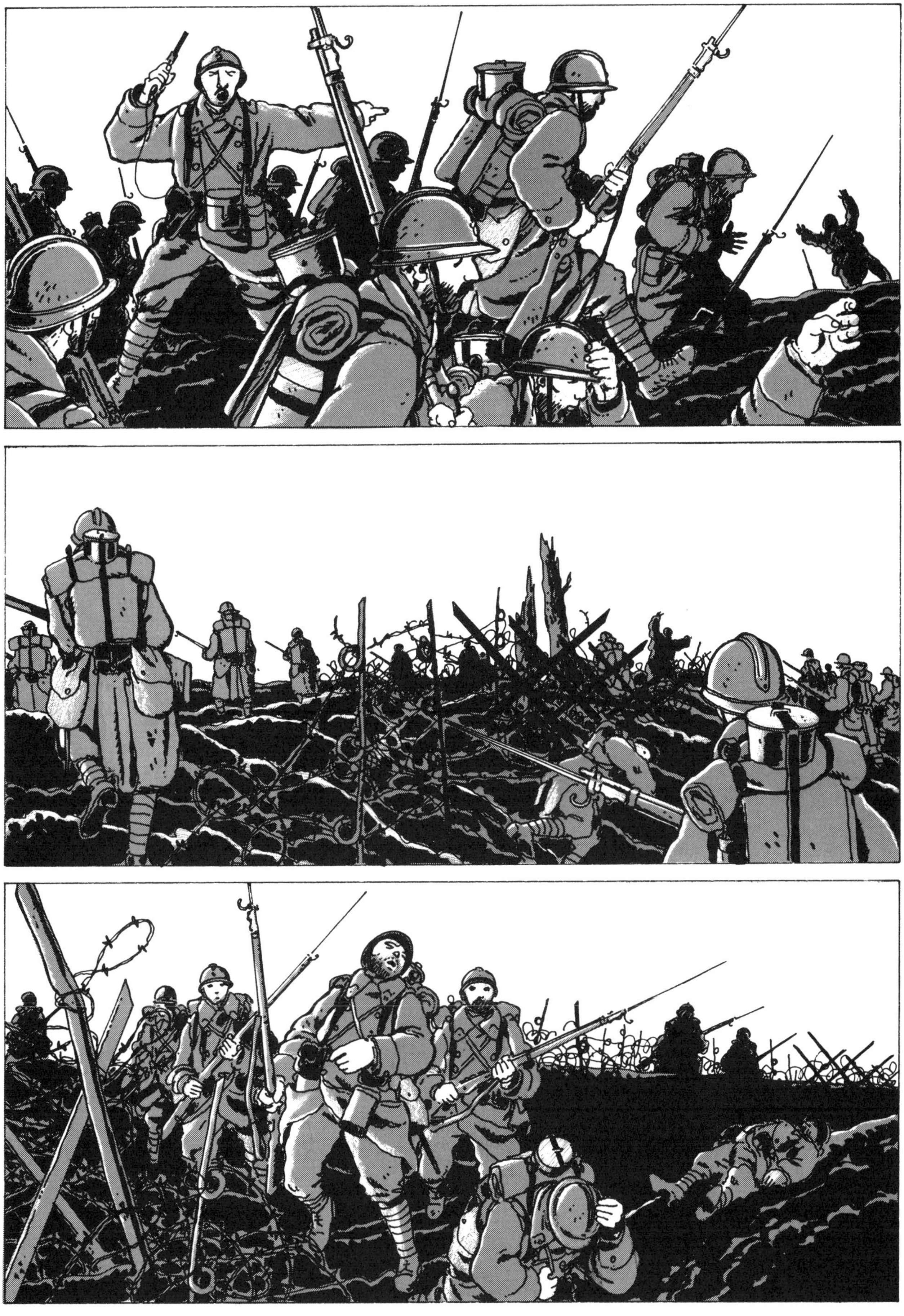

"Joyful, despite their grief, are those families whose blood flows for their country." (General REBILLOT, *Libre Parole*, December 13, 1914.)

"Go forth, little soldier! Your exhaustion, your wounds, your out-cast's terror, even your death, all beyond price. We will pity you, we will love you, and if God so wishes, we will mourn you.., We will proclaim, with heaven our witness: Died on the battlefield." (Abbé SERTILLANGES, *Madeleine*, September 14 1914.)

BASTARDS, BASTARDS, MISERABLE FUCKING BASTARDS! FUCK THE ARMY! FRANCE CAN KISS MY ASS!

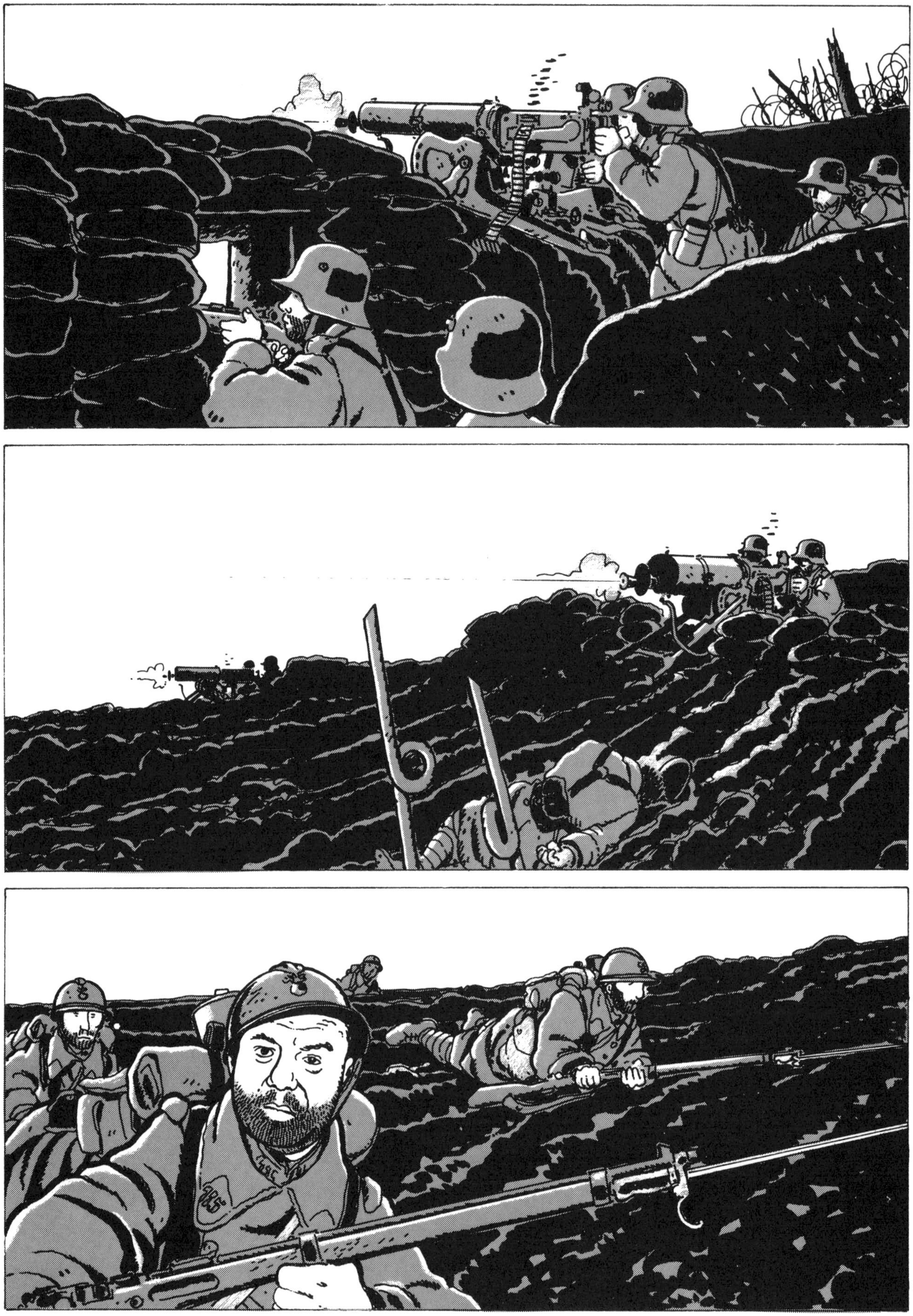

The men retreated to the trench they'd come from.

Exhausted, the survivors from the 3rd Company collapse into the trench. For the third time in forty-eight hours, their charge has been broken. Demoralized, haggard, and disgusted, having lost all will to fight, they seek shelter. Out of one hundred and twenty men, only sixty-three have regained the French lines.

Immediately upon their return the soldiers are subjected to intense shelling.

There's not much left of the 3rd Company. The offensive was a failure, just like yesterday's. Our Captain was killed, we rejoined our lines, and now our artillery has started shelling us. We're being killed by our own side. This isn't the first time our cannons've shot short and we've taken it up the ass!

Brigadier General BERTHIER. It is no accident that our artillery is now pounding the trench to which the 3rd company has retreated. It was I who gave the order. The men turned tail, the cowards retreated, they fled when faced with the enemy. The objective they had been given was crucial. We must overrun the *Boche* positions before December, cost be damned. It is part of our plans for the winter offensive. By shooting at the 3rd Company, I want to force the men to re-emerge in order to begin the assault anew.

But the soldiers did not re-emerge. At six o'clock, the artillery fire ceased. General BERTHIER decided to have the entire Company shot. A Colonel attempted to save his men, pleading exhaustion on their part.

The 3rd Company was taken to a village at the rear.

General BERTHIER decided that the execution of three men would satisfy him. They were picked at random by the platoon commanders. They were court-martialed and sentenced to die by firing squad. Private Jean DESBOIS was among them...

43.

Kneeling in front of a barn, with no stakes and blind-folded, the condemned men were shot by young soldiers who had recently arrived at the front.

The entire regiment witnessed the execution of the three soldiers.

The war continued...

SOUFFLOT had given it a lot of thought. Someone had clued him in to the scam three months earlier... He'd heard about it from a private who hadn't tried it himself but who'd told him it never failed. After all, that private had heard it from another fellow who knew a guy who'd pulled it off.

So SOUFFLOT had thought it over and made his decision; he was resolute. He pulled from his haversack a needle and sewing thread and rolled up his left sleeve, then he worked the thread between his teeth to remove the bits of food.

Using the needle, he poked the thread covered in refuse into the skin of his arm. The pain was piercing, but he persevered.

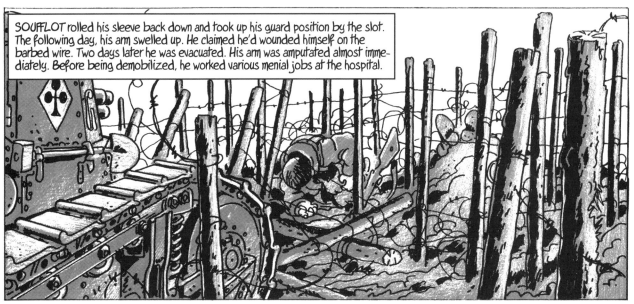

SOUFFLOT rolled his sleeve back down and took up his guard position by the slot. The following day, his arm swelled up. He claimed he'd wounded himself on the barbed wire. Two days later he was evacuated. His arm was amputated almost immediately. Before being demobilized, he worked various menial jobs at the hospital.

SOUFFLOT mailed, in a little iron container, a piece of his gangrenous dressing to his friend GRUMEAU, who cut open his thigh and rolled a bandage around it to hold it in place. GRUMEAU was as desperate as SOUFFLOT must have been, but he died very shortly thereafter, the gangrene spreading to his groin and his belly with terrifying speed.

Seeking work in Paris, SOUFFLOT was not yet aware of GRUMEAU's death. He could no longer work his old job. What would he be able to do? It wasn't his invalid veteran's pay that was going to keep him going. He ordered an Amer-Picon... Meanwhile, the war continued.

"First of all, I must say this right off, I never could stand the countryside. I always found it depressing, with its endless stretches of mud, its perpetually deserted houses, and its roads that lead nowhere. Add war to the mix, though, and it becomes unbearable." (L.-F. Céline, *Voyage to the End of Night*.)

Oct. 12, 1916...

Alone at the slot, trench fever raging through his body, Private HUET thought back to a summer day,

It was very early on in the war, on the Belgian side, perhaps even in Belgium proper...

There were real corpses in the fields...

...Dead horses blown up by the sun, big as elephants, and villages destroyed by real shells.

We were marching, dazed by the heat, our feet aching from the new boots.

We were crossing civilians, fleeing the combat sites toward which we were headed.

I would have liked to follow them, but we were going in exactly the opposite direction.

Resting, we were passed by a platoon of dragoons. They, too, were headed straight for trouble.

Then it was back to the road, the dust and heat, the increasing agony of the march, our kidneys crushed by the sixty or so pounds of equipment we were lugging.

Our proud dragoons had come this way...

We came across two pointmen on horseback, sent on reconnaissance. The Germans were not far, just a few kilometers.

So we were given the order to deploy as a skirmish contingent in the fields, on either side of the road.

I was advancing with the others, protecting my belly with the butt of the rifle. We'd heard the Germans were using dum-dum bullets.

Then a soldier shot at a man who was advancing toward us.

It turned out to be a grenadier from the Belgian army who'd been mistaken for an enemy soldier because of his baker's cap, similar to the one worn by the Germans.

We had no time to discuss this "incident" amongst ourselves because other retreating Belgians arrived on the scene...

They told us the Germans were coming up the road. They had just left, after setting it on fire, the village that could be seen burning at the edge of the fields.

We were ordered to take our positions in the ditch by the road.

I was there with these men I didn't know, clutching my rifle, and I was afraid. I wanted to go home and I was also ashamed that I was readying myself to kill. I was ashamed for myself and for the others...

But the Germans had a nasty surprise in store for us.

Suddenly we understood why the Belgians had been retreating. The Germans were advancing, preceded by the women and children of the village.

But we were French and they were not. We were given the order to shoot into the advancing group.

54.

HUET remembered that summer day quite clearly, what had happened on the road, and the ensuing carnage. The women throwing themselves onto the ground, the Germans firing. He was in the ditch with the others, he didn't even remember the outcome of the battle. All he knew was that he'd used his rifle. He'd seen the young woman fall, the one who was holding two children by their hands.

For the last two years, whether in the trench or in the shelter, he'd been seeing them over and over, her and the two kids, he saw them falling again...

SAPE 15

At times, he thought maybe he hadn't killed her, so confusing had the shooting been, but there were other times when he was convinced that he'd committed this act of murder.

55.

His doubts magnified his fears and he was sinking slowly into madness, like this October night under the rain, alone at the slot, eaten alive by fever, with the girl and the two kids staring at him.

HUET couldn't take it any more — it was too much to endure. He climbed over the edge of the trench.

And deliberately, slowly, he began walking toward the German position...

He had made his decision; he knew Helmut would be there that evening.

He reached the tangle of barbed wire.

Did Helmut want him to advance farther still? What was the dirty *Boche* waiting for?

Helmut calmly took aim at his target, realizing that this was as close as the Frenchman could advance, due to the barbed wire. It bothered him that HUET was not carrying a rifle. But maybe he had grenades. He pressed the trigger.

HUET took the bullet right in his stomach. He'd always dreaded that kind of wound, but as it turned out, he was killed almost instantaneously.

He fell to his knees, his body stuck to the barbed wire in a ridiculous position. He saw the girl and the kids one final time. Then he saw no more...

One week later...

HUET's corpse was rotting, a few meters from the trench. The men were complaining about the stench, they found it unbearable even though they had become accustomed to it.

Captain, Sir!

Sergeant... Get rid of Private HUET's corpse... Send a man. Have him bury him on the spot. The sight of this corpse is not good for the company's morale! That's an order!

The Sergeant selected AKERMANN and handed him a pair of clippers.

AKERMANN didn't stand a chance against Helmut in daylight. He knew it, and the Captain knew it.

Helmut calmly lined up his target and waited for the soldier to reach the corpse before he took his shot.

That same morning, the Captain had received a forty-eight-hour leave for Private AKERMANN, which had not prevented him from telling the Sergeant, "Send the Jewboy!"

Aug. 29, 1914.

MAZURE hadn't seen much of the battle.,, Just the Germans, so close in the field, that was it.,, He'd felt a sharp pain in his side and ended up on all fours in the grass.,, There'd been noise, too, and cannon fire; these gigantic goddamned horses had almost trampled him.

MAZURE had lost his rifle and had ditched his haversack to go hide out in the little forest he'd spotted just before the *Boches* had descended upon them.

In the woods, he'd run into the German officer who was expiring among the leaves.,, The fucker had tried to kill him but MAZURE had managed to take away his weapon.

The battle appeared to be winding down. The other guy, who hadn't gotten around to kicking the bucket, had started yelling. After a moment's hesitation MAZURE, to keep the noise down, had taken the German's saber and plunged it into his belly.

No one was paying attention to this little corner, and MAZURE wanted to keep the war away from it.

The battle had ended and night had fallen.

He wanted to leave but didn't know in which direction he should go. Had the French army advanced? Lately it had mostly been the Germans who'd been gaining ground. Which way had MAZURE come from? In the darkness, it was impossible to tell.., He stiffened, woozy, in pain, fear pouring off his body.

Later, he had tried to stand up. This had reminded him that his flank was on fire.

He managed to get out of the woods by crawling on his knees.

He hadn't gone 50 feet before he vomited the entire contents of his stomach.

Then, twisting his ankles in the furrows and avoiding the corpses, MAZURE walked across the battlefield, which he was in a hurry to leave far behind. Wounded men were screaming.

Out of fear, he had pissed his britches.

Dawn was breaking as he arrived in the village.

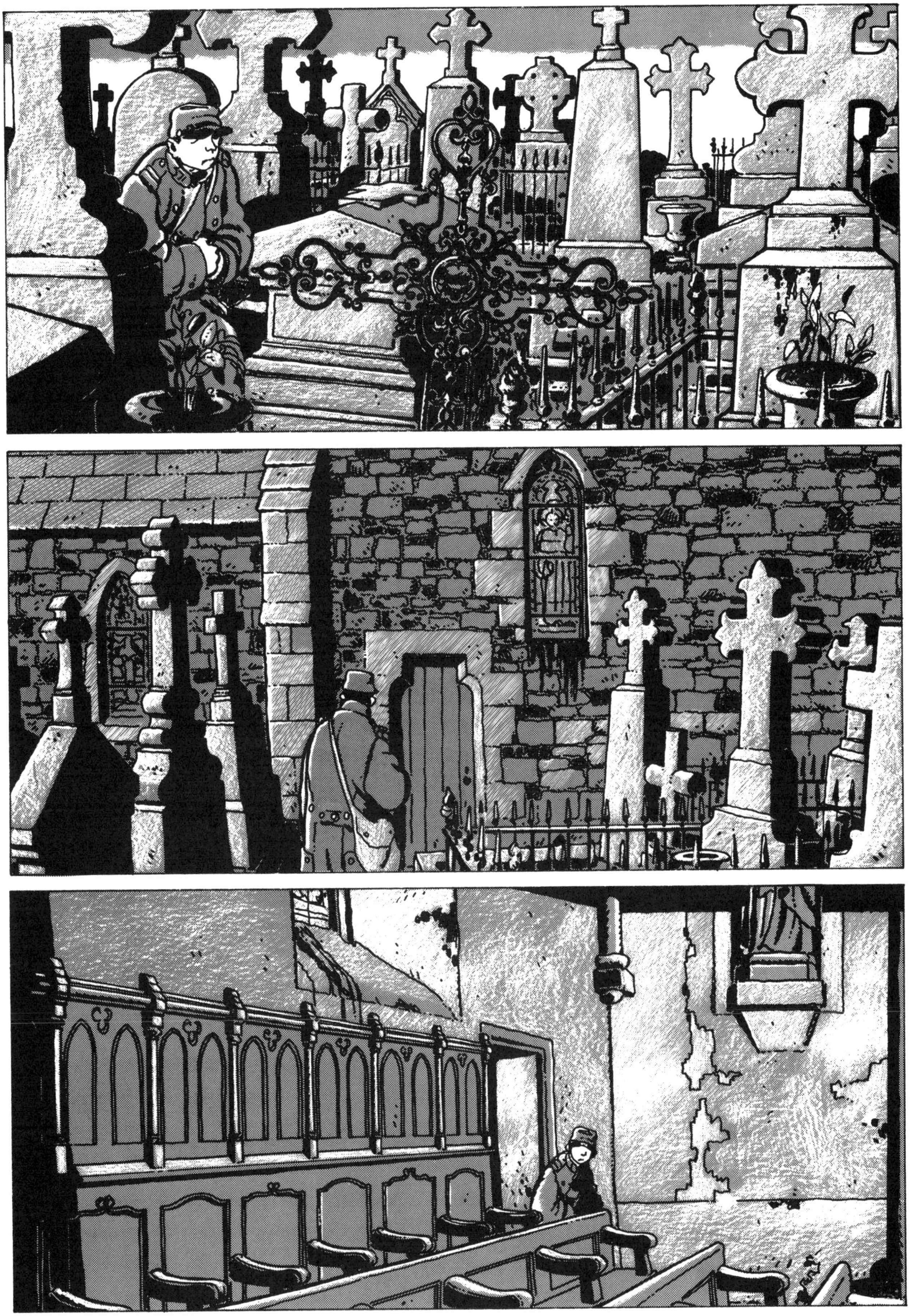

It had been a long time since MAZURE had been in a church. He was surprised to find himself there...

...There was nothing but corpses.

MAZURE couldn't believe it: There he was, stretched out on the cellar floor. The last thing he remembered seeing: The two cavalry-men, bled white like hogs, ashen, covered in mud... and now there was the *Boche*'s face, staring right at him...

...brandishing the enormous gun that he, MAZURE, had lifted from the officer in the woods. The German must have found it in his haversack. But what the hell was he doing here, that big Kraut bastard? Surely he was getting a kick out of playing with the Mauser, he had to be getting ready to use it...

Now you are my prisoner, little Froggy.

MAZURE's side was hurting, of course, but he was pretty pleased at the idea that the war was over for him... It had lasted long enough to suit him. He was tempted to kiss him, the German. His name was Werner.

He'd misjudged him right off the bat; the German wasn't such a bad fellow after all. He'd been hiding out in the cellar for four days now, living off the eggs from the chickens and what he'd scrounged in the surrounding houses. He'd lost his regiment and didn't know which direction to take. Werner had told MAZURE his whole story. His French was quite good; he'd been a bellboy for a hotel in Nice in earlier times.

That morning, the two cavalrymen had showed up. They'd surprised Werner in the church, and he'd taken them out. He'd hidden the horses and had come back to get rid of the bodies, he'd run across MAZURE, he'd knocked him out and dragged him down into the cellar. He hadn't killed him... He had something up his sleeve.

What Werner had in mind was that they'd both lost their way, that they basically were brothers in trouble. If the Germans ended up taking the territory, then MAZURE would be the prisoner. If it turned out the other way around, Werner would be MAZURE's prisoner. He was proposing an arrangement, a deal that would work both ways. All they had to do was wait, that way they didn't have to murder one another.

It was like a game. The basement window looked out onto the village square; there was no way they would miss whoever might show up. The unlucky one in this story would be given a medal for sure: a hero for having captured the lucky bastard who was now done with this crummy jaunt in the country...

Two German hussars, certainly on recon-naissance, showed up in the afternoon.

Werner and MAZURE had stayed down in the cellar, dithering, indecisive, not knowing what to do. They were hesitating as if suddenly unsure of their scheme.

The hussars had been gone for a while and they still felt just as discombobulated.

That evening, the town was pounded with shells for a full hour. The half-destroyed village had been occupied by the Germans. There had been fighting, and then it had been abandoned. Who was doing the shooting? That was what MAZURE and the German were wondering, hiding in their hole...

At dawn, a handful of French soldiers on reconnaissance strode into the deserted, now smoking village. They took up positions and the rest of their regiment followed, complete with General and staff, all present and accounted for. The village, in which there were no enemies to be found, had just fallen into the hands of the French.

Every house was inspected, searched from top to bottom.

Then a soldier broke into the cellar...

...He saw the German and fired!

MAZURE had found his regiment again, the 71st... He thought to himself that if it was just two of you, you could make peace, anything beyond that, it was fucked... He was going to have to rejoin the war. His side was hurting him more and more.

At 3 o'clock the War Council met in the village schoolroom. MAZURE was judged and sentenced for abandoning his post when facing the enemy, and sharing intelligence with the latter... A deserter, basically, who'd spent forty-eight hours fraternizing with a German who had done nothing to him and whom he had no reason to wish ill... MAZURE did not hear a word of the sentence. The rifle blast in the cellar had deafened him... He was executed the following morning, stood up against the cemetery wall.

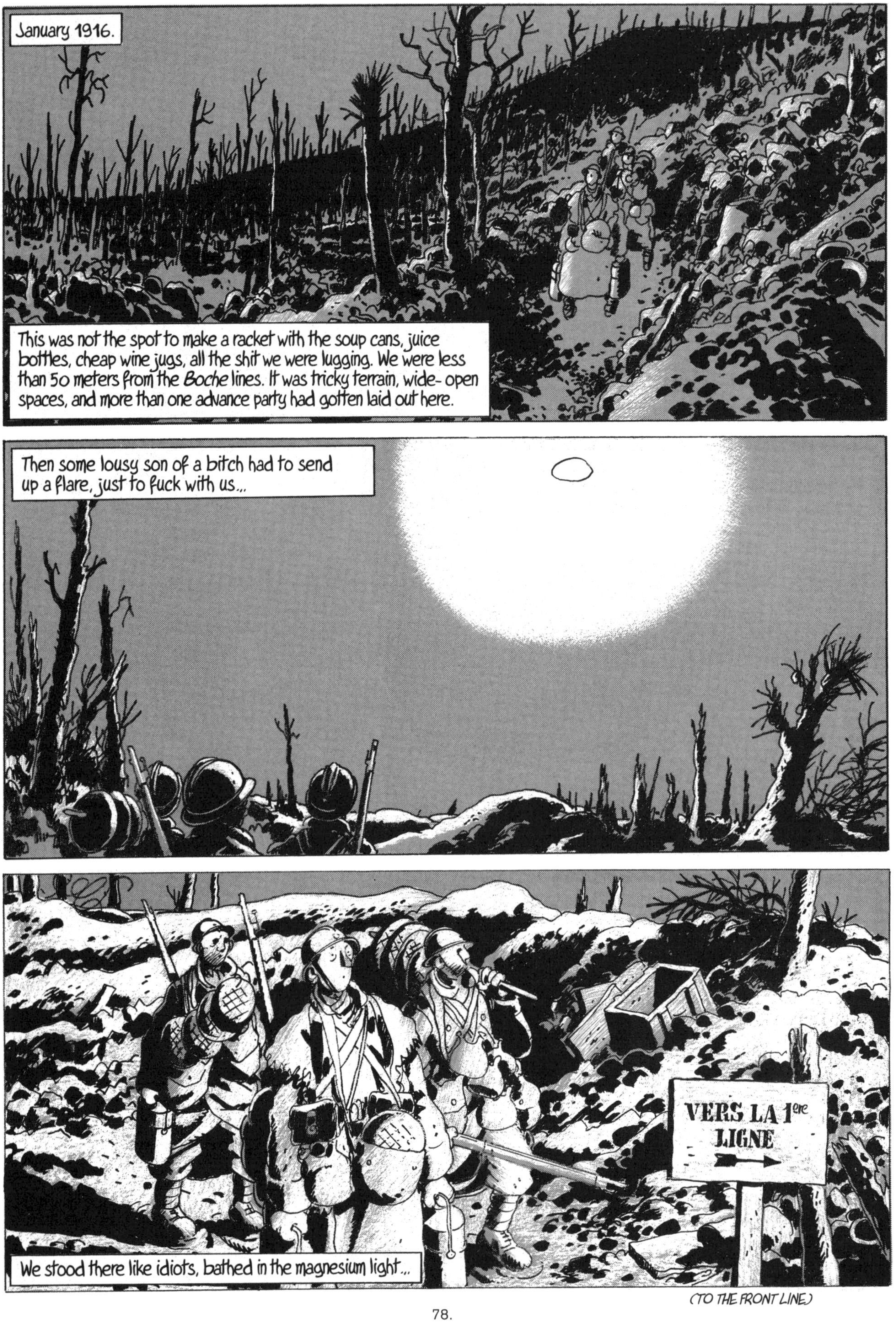
January 1916.
This was not the spot to make a racket with the soup cans, juice bottles, cheap wine jugs, all the shit we were lugging. We were less than 50 meters from the *Boche* lines. It was tricky terrain, wide- open spaces, and more than one advance party had gotten laid out here.
Then some lousy son of a bitch had to send up a flare, just to fuck with us...
VERS LA 1ère LIGNE
We stood there like idiots, bathed in the magnesium light...

(TO THE FRONT LINE)

It didn't take long for a gunner to get us in his sights.

Raoul and *Li'l Louis* went down, shot dead, and I ended up wrist deep in the *Boche*'s entrails.

My greatest fear was gangrene... I looked for a puddle to wash off in. After walking in circles for a while I got lost. The shooting had stopped, it was peaceful again, but I had no idea which way to go.

I walked on, hiding as best I could behind the trees, until I reached a village I wasn't familiar with. I thought about what an amazing amount of plumbing a man carries around in his belly, and how fragile the envelope that protects it all is... Our bodies really hadn't been created to withstand the barrage of metal that's being flung at us!

The village I'd ended up in wasn't exactly a barrel of laughs... Not to mention that there might be *Boches* hiding in the ruins.

I was begining to wonder if I hadn't seriously fucked up by taking this road... It looked like Main Street had been the scene of a major clash...

And then I came across the gendarmes, two of them, all laid out... both of them military police.

MORT AUX VACHES

BOUCHERIE

Those two didn't die heroes or anything like that, just so y'know.

**?**

...Nearly shot you!

A sight for sore eyes, ain't it?

What the fuck're you doin' here?

Oh, just takin' it all in!

BOUCHERIE

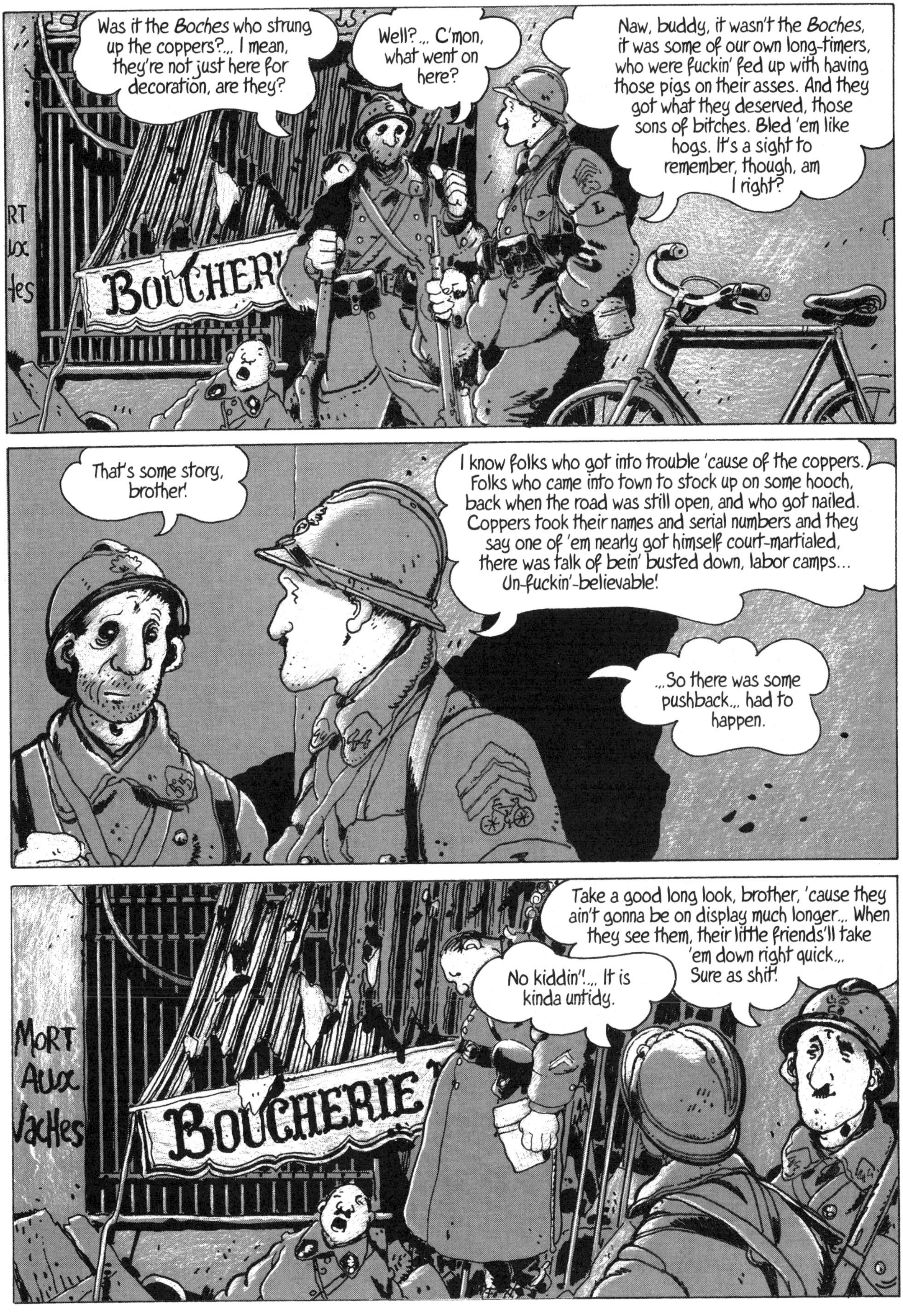
Was it the Boches who strung up the coppers?... I mean, they're not just here for decoration, are they?
Well?... C'mon, what went on here?
Naw, buddy, it wasn't the Boches, it was some of our own long-timers, who were fuckin' fed up with having those pigs on their asses. And they got what they deserved, those sons of bitches. Bled 'em like hogs. It's a sight to remember, though, am I right?
BOUCHER
That's some story, brother!
I know folks who got into trouble 'cause of the coppers. Folks who came into town to stock up on some hooch, back when the road was still open, and who got nailed. Coppers took their names and serial numbers and they say one of 'em nearly got himself court-martialed, there was talk of bein' busted down, labor camps... Un-fuckin'-believable!
...So there was some pushback... had to happen.
Take a good long look, brother, 'cause they ain't gonna be on display much longer... When they see them, their little friends'll take 'em down right quick... Sure as shit!
No kiddin'!... It is kinda untidy.
MORT AUX VACHES
BOUCHERIE

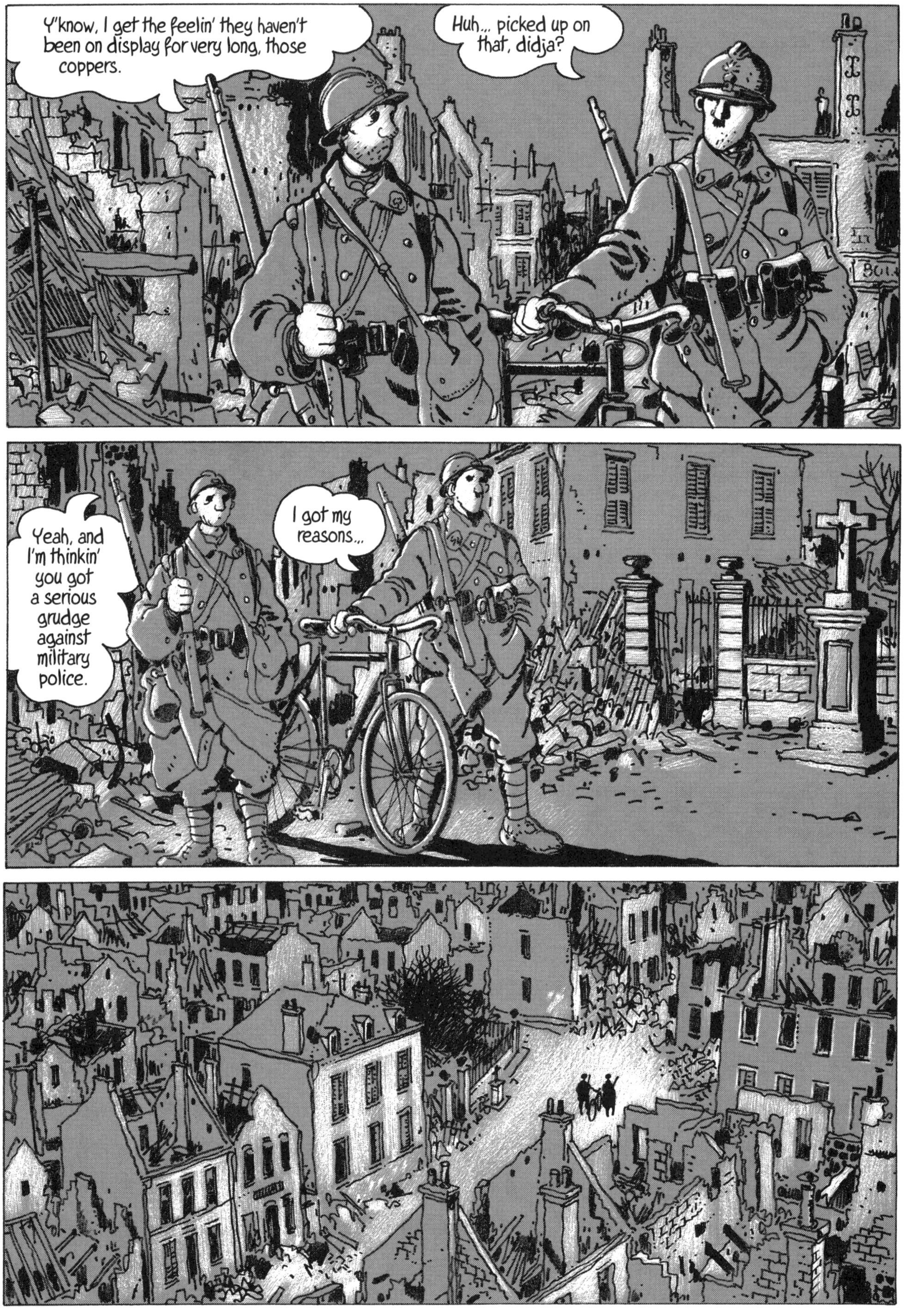
Y'know, I get the feelin' they haven't been on display for very long, those coppers.
Huh... picked up on that, didja?
Yeah, and I'm thinkin' you got a serious grudge against military police.
I got my reasons...

AAAA
...Where'd you go, shithead?... Can't move...

...Can't feel my back... Oh fuck, it fuckin' hurts!... What's wrong with me?... Help me get back up...

The coppers... That was you, wasn't it?

Yeah!... Go ahead and rat me out to JOFFRE if you want... while you're at it, tell 'im to go fuck himself!!...

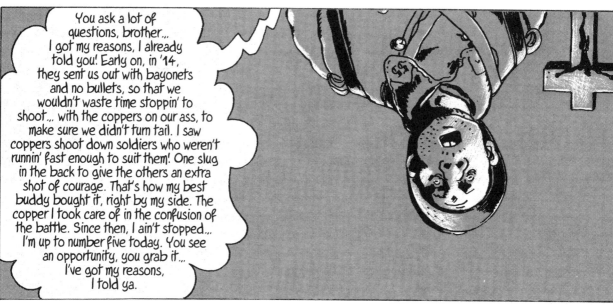

You ask a lot of questions, brother... I got my reasons, I already told you! Early on, in '14, they sent us out with bayonets and no bullets, so that we wouldn't waste time stoppin' to shoot... with the coppers on our ass, to make sure we didn't turn tail. I saw coppers shoot down soldiers who weren't runnin' fast enough to suit them! One slug in the back to give the others an extra shot of courage. That's how my best buddy bought it, right by my side. The copper I took care of in the confusion of the battle. Since then, I ain't stopped... I'm up to number five today. You see an opportunity, you grab it... I've got my reasons, I told ya.

Shit, my leg, it's bent all the way back, all fucked up... I guess that bicycle I found's a goner, and all the rest of it... What d'you make of a religion that promotes itself with a naked guy who's been tortured and nailed to two pieces of wood?...

Nothin' good!

Is that something we oughta be showin' children?... What's gonna happen to my own li'l brats now, huh?... You got an answer for that?... Nobody ever thinks of that when we get ourselves killed. You think the coppers got kids?

"Mommy"... Those were his last words. He was beyond crazy, the guy with the bicycle, dangerous, too... I took his piece so it wouldn't fall into enemy hands, regulations, you know... We were short on the rifles we needed to keep the killing going.

I walked past my scarecrow again. Amazing how much harm it was possible to inflict on men and beasts... On men, fine, it was their war, after all.

I paused for a minute before slipping into the trench. There'd been bloodshed, it seemed abandoned, not kept up... the last few days' thunderstorms hadn't helped things either.

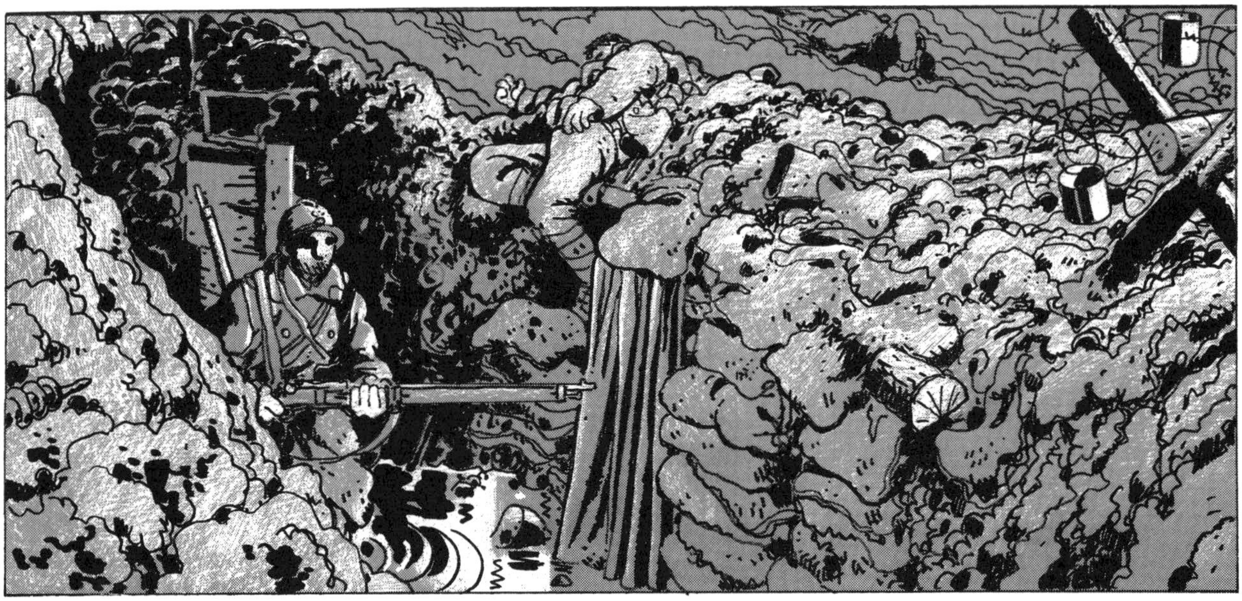

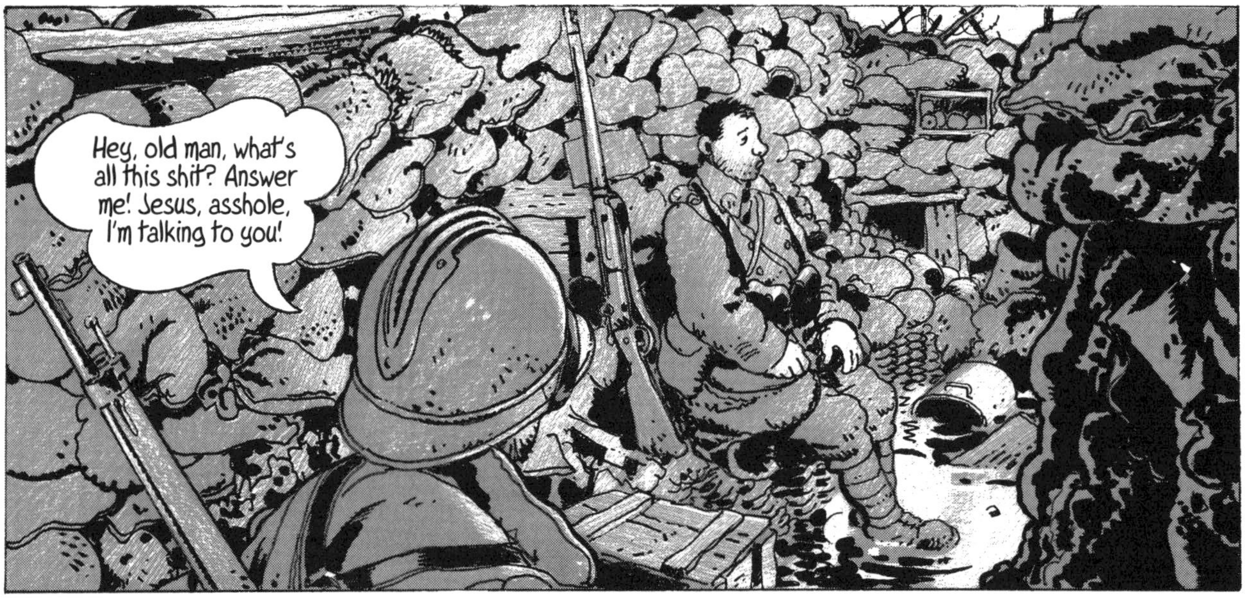
Hey, old man, what's all this shit? Answer me! Jesus, asshole, I'm talking to you!

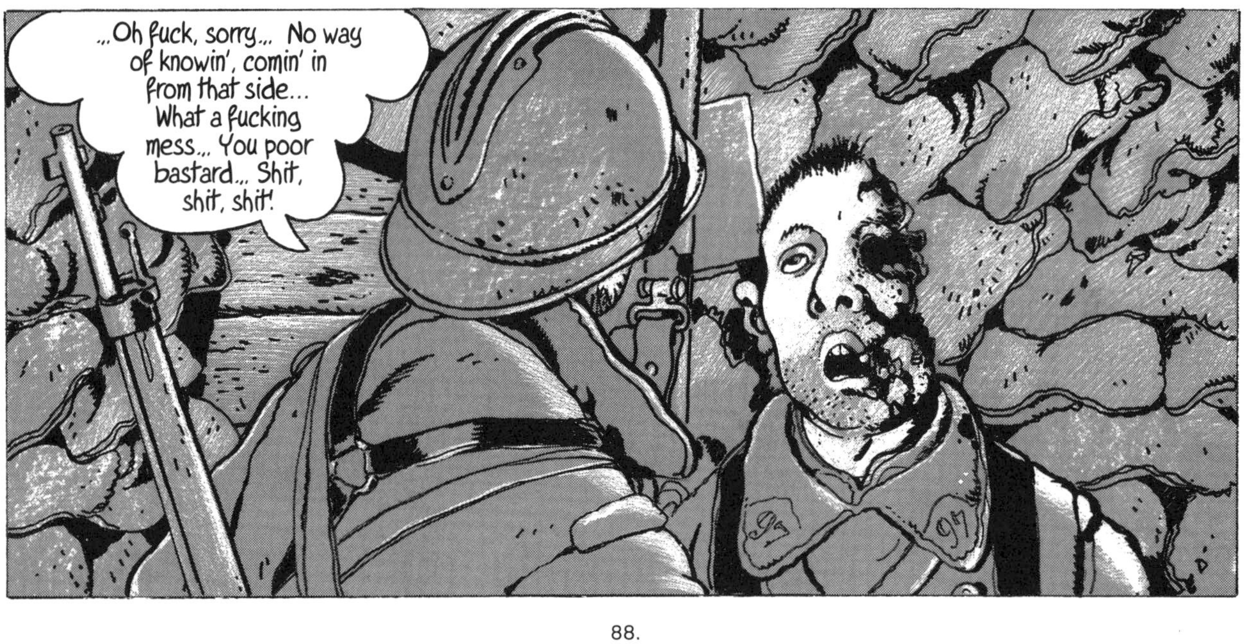
...Oh fuck, sorry... No way of knowin', comin' in from that side... What a fucking mess... You poor bastard... Shit, shit, shit!

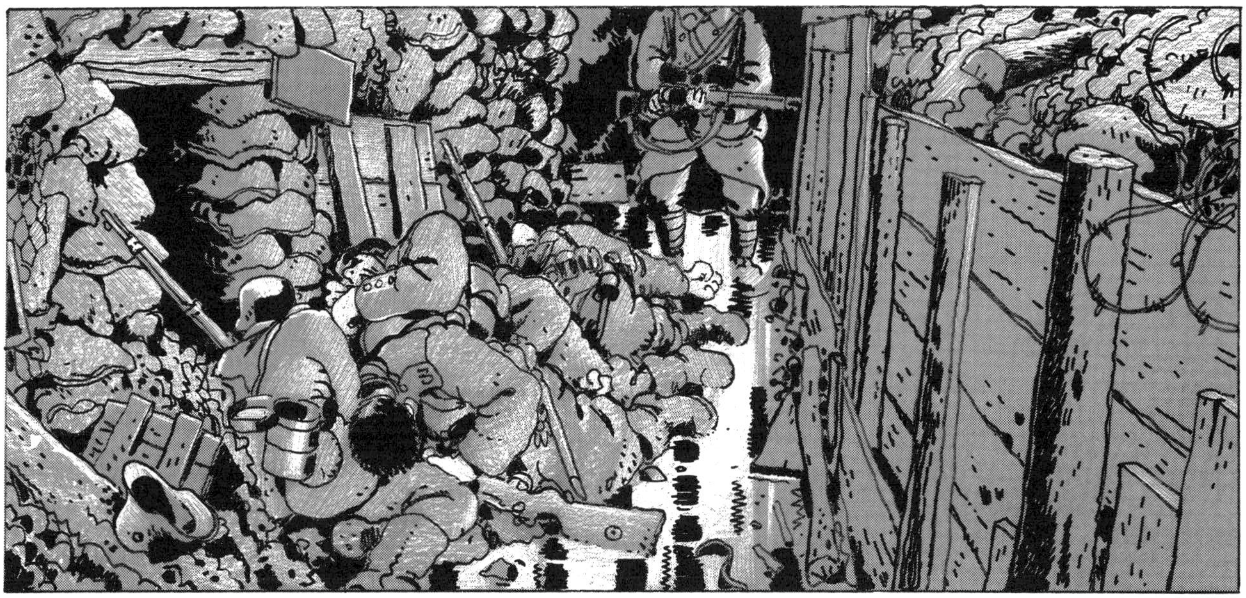

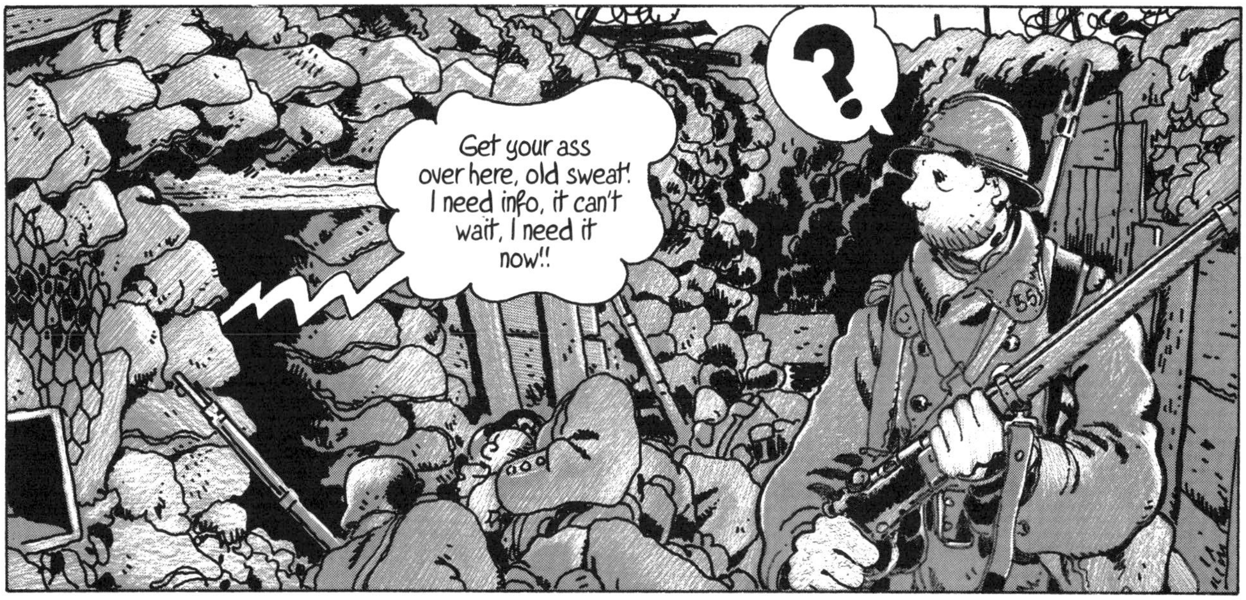
?
Get your ass over here, old sweat! I need info, it can't wait, I need it now!!

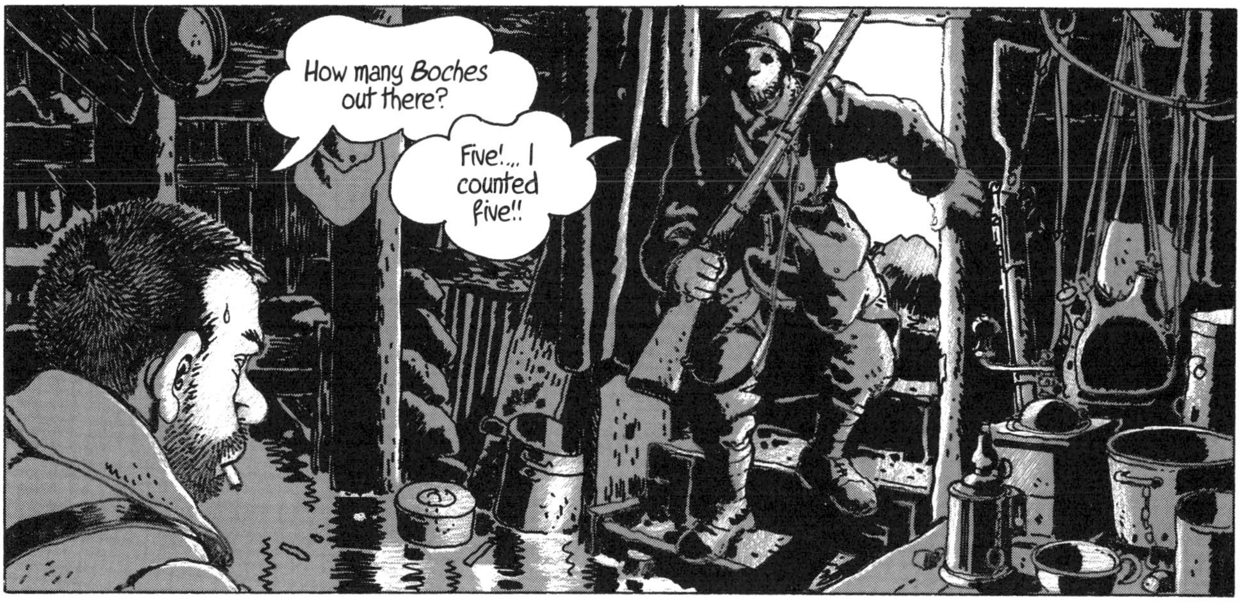
How many *Boches* out there?
Five!... I counted five!!

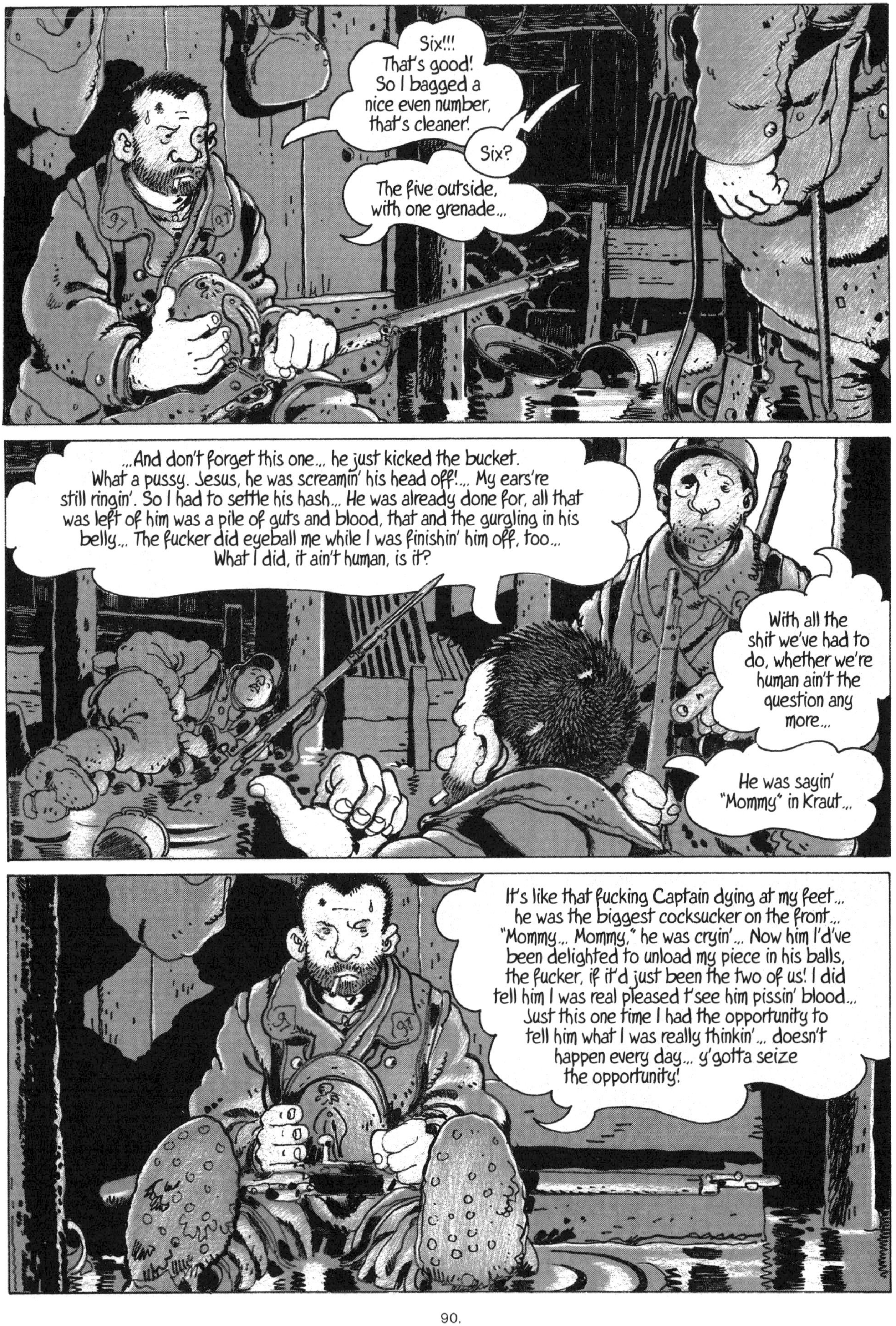
Six!!! That's good! So I bagged a nice even number, that's cleaner!
Six?
The five outside, with one grenade...
...And don't forget this one... he just kicked the bucket. What a pussy. Jesus, he was screamin' his head off!... My ears're still ringin'. So I had to settle his hash... He was already done for, all that was left of him was a pile of guts and blood, that and the gurgling in his belly... The fucker did eyeball me while I was finishin' him off, too... What I did, it ain't human, is it?
With all the shit we've had to do, whether we're human ain't the question any more...
He was sayin' "Mommy" in Kraut...
It's like that fucking Captain dying at my feet... he was the biggest cocksucker on the front... "Mommy... Mommy," he was cryin'... Now him I'd've been delighted to unload my piece in his balls, the fucker, if it'd just been the two of us! I did tell him I was real pleased t'see him pissin' blood... Just this one time I had the opportunity to tell him what I was really thinkin'... doesn't happen every day... y'gotta seize the opportunity!

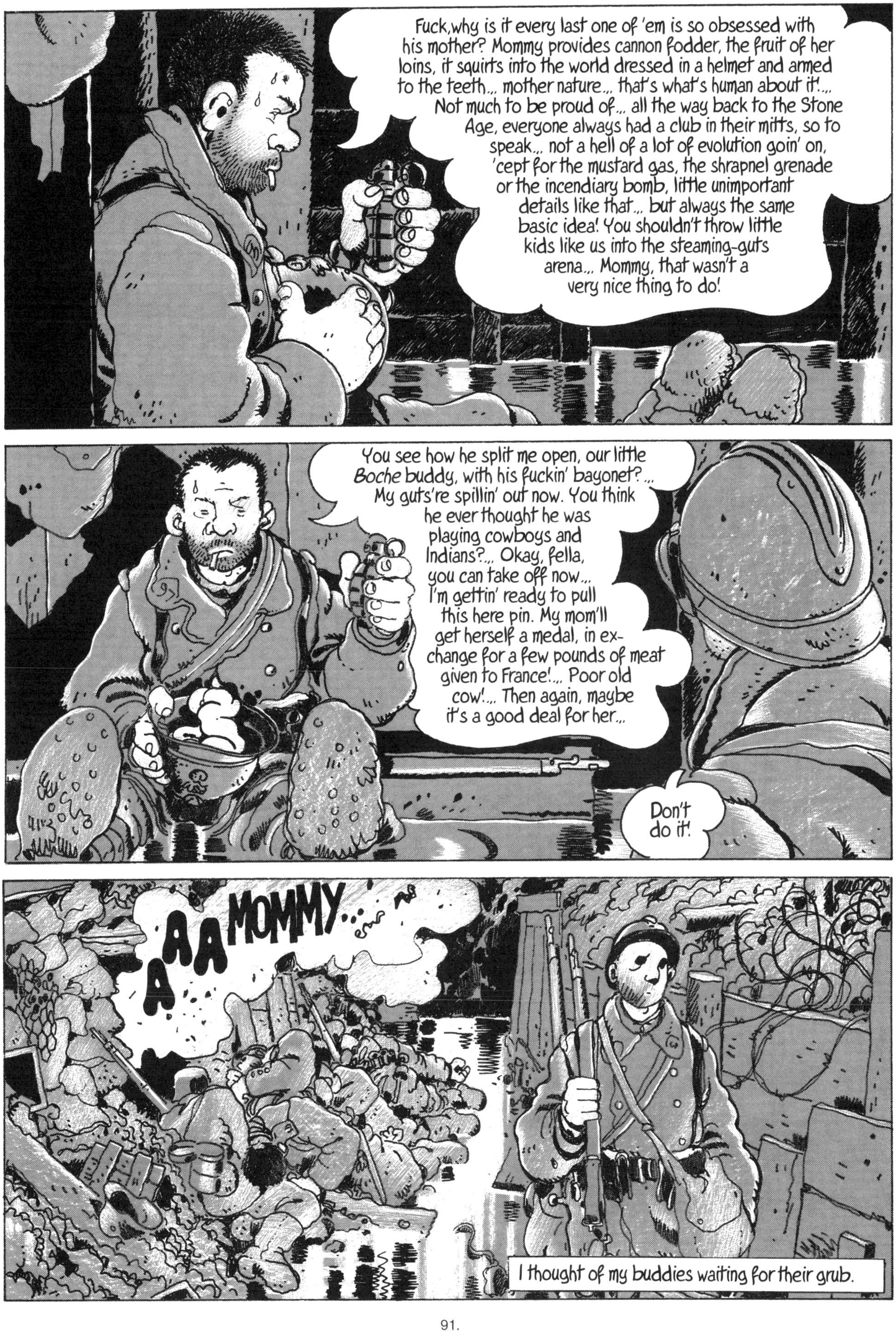
Fuck, why is it every last one of 'em is so obsessed with his mother? Mommy provides cannon fodder, the fruit of her loins, it squirts into the world dressed in a helmet and armed to the teeth... mother nature... that's what's human about it!... Not much to be proud of... all the way back to the Stone Age, everyone always had a club in their mitts, so to speak... not a hell of a lot of evolution goin' on, 'cept for the mustard gas, the shrapnel grenade or the incendiary bomb, little unimportant details like that... but always the same basic idea! You shouldn't throw little kids like us into the steaming-guts arena... Mommy, that wasn't a very nice thing to do!
You see how he split me open, our little *Boche* buddy, with his fuckin' bayonet?... My guts're spillin' out now. You think he ever thought he was playing cowboys and Indians?... Okay, fella, you can take off now... I'm gettin' ready to pull this here pin. My mom'll get herself a medal, in exchange for a few pounds of meat given to France!... Poor old cow!... Then again, maybe it's a good deal for her...
Don't do it!
AAAMOMMY...
I thought of my buddies waiting for their grub.

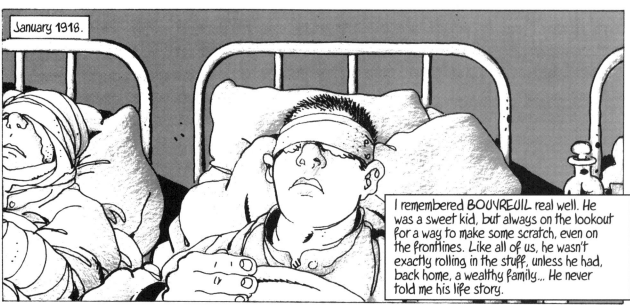

I remembered BOUVREUIL real well. He was a sweet kid, but always on the lookout for a way to make some scratch, even on the frontlines. Like all of us, he wasn't exactly rolling in the stuff, unless he had, back home, a wealthy family... He never told me his life story.

It's shapin' up! Sweet, innit?

It's a beaut!

Anyway, BOUVREUIL was some kind of artist. He spent his downtime sitting on his ass working his copper bits and pieces, chopping up scrap to make souvenirs and money. Because he was always in a good mood and utterly disarming, even though he was on the rough side, we kept him supplied with materials.

As soon as one of us scored a shell casing, he'd give it to him to make a vase, and BOUVREUIL would work the metal on demand, creating the requested designs, in exchange for a couple of coins.

That came out real purty, that ring did... my gal's gonna be happy!

Like it?... Five francs! Solid alumi- num...

Y'oughta get yourself a smaller one, unless your girl's got big ol' sausage fingers like yours...

He had a special bag where he had all sorts of tools and on command he could create a wide variety of objects, from a Verdun letter-opener to an artillery-shell inkwell, including the Kaiser's ugly mug on a pig's body, a silhouette carved from a German artillery fragment, painstakingly pounded into shape.

Prince Asshole's old man... looks just like 'im, too!

Five francs!

Under his hands, the bullets became crucifixes or pen holders. BOUVRIER was like an ammo silversmith... that was why we were so fond of him.

I need a volunteer for the little outpost!

You got all your gear, PRUNIER?!... C'mon, go relieve FOUR-NEAU, he's gotta be gettin' impatient...

Pick someone else! I got my leave in my pocket, I'm takin' the train out tonight... Six days without seeing your ugly mug!... I'd love to help you out, but find yourself another sucker.

How much if I go instead?

Work it out, you two!

93.

BOUVREUIL put away his tools and locked PRUNIER's fiver in the "Muratti's after lunch" iron box where he kept his stash.

Watch my stuff, fellas... PRUNIER, give yer fiancée a smooch from me!

Sure. Be careful.

Then he vanished into the tunnel that led to the observation post, less than fifty meters from the German lines.

We were watching BOUVREUIL because there was a bad patch — one the *Boches* were pretty familiar with — where you had to run out in the open before leaping into the little outpost. We'd never been able to dig it out, because of an enemy machine gun that guarded it... which made it real dangerous to go there in daytime, but there was no other access. We hoped like Hell that "FRITZ" had moved away from his gun, to have himself a wurst... for BOUVREUIL's sake.

94.

FOURNEAU'd gotten wasted...

...And, in fact, "FRITZ" had not abandoned his popgun to eat his wurst.

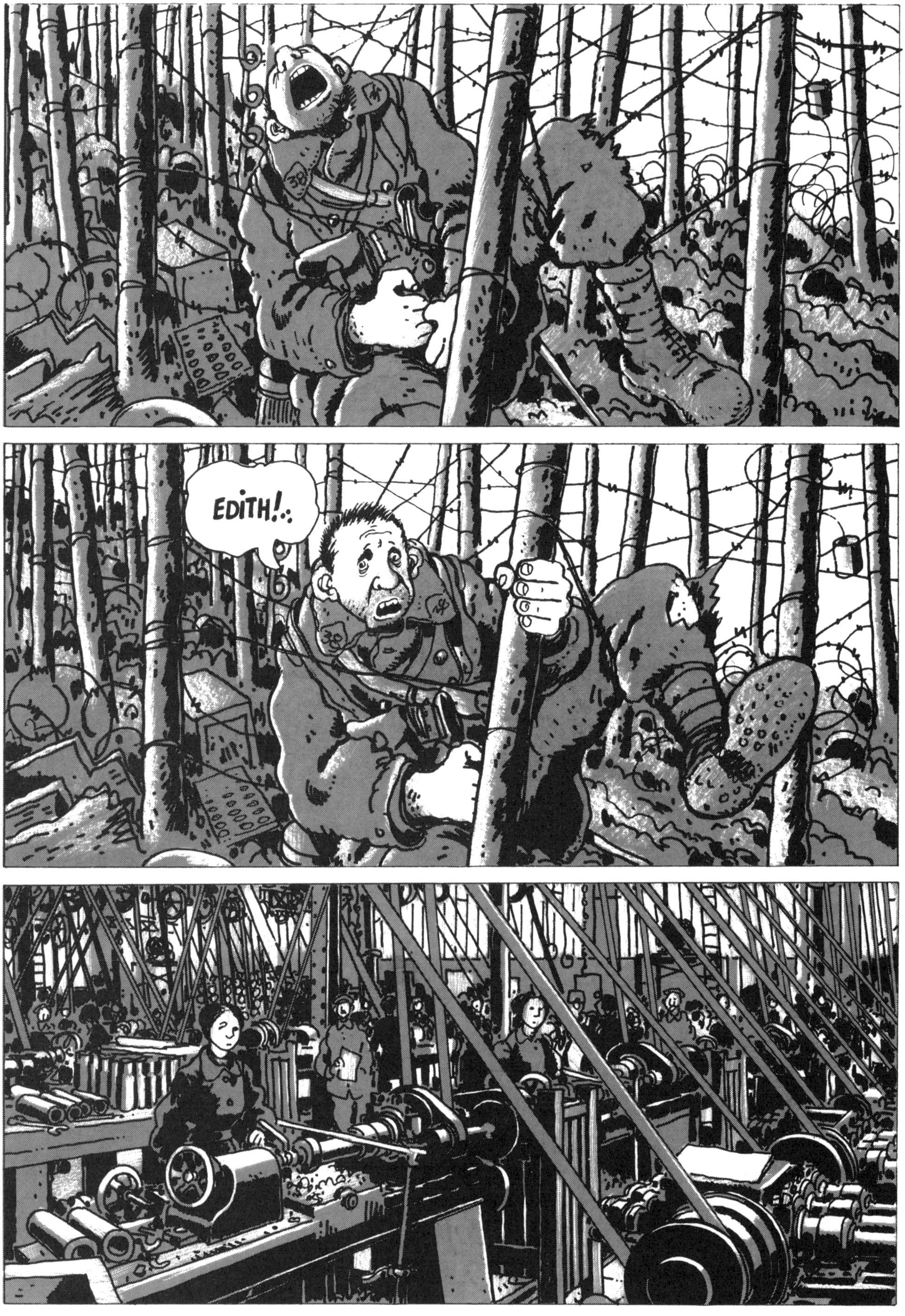
EDITH!.:.

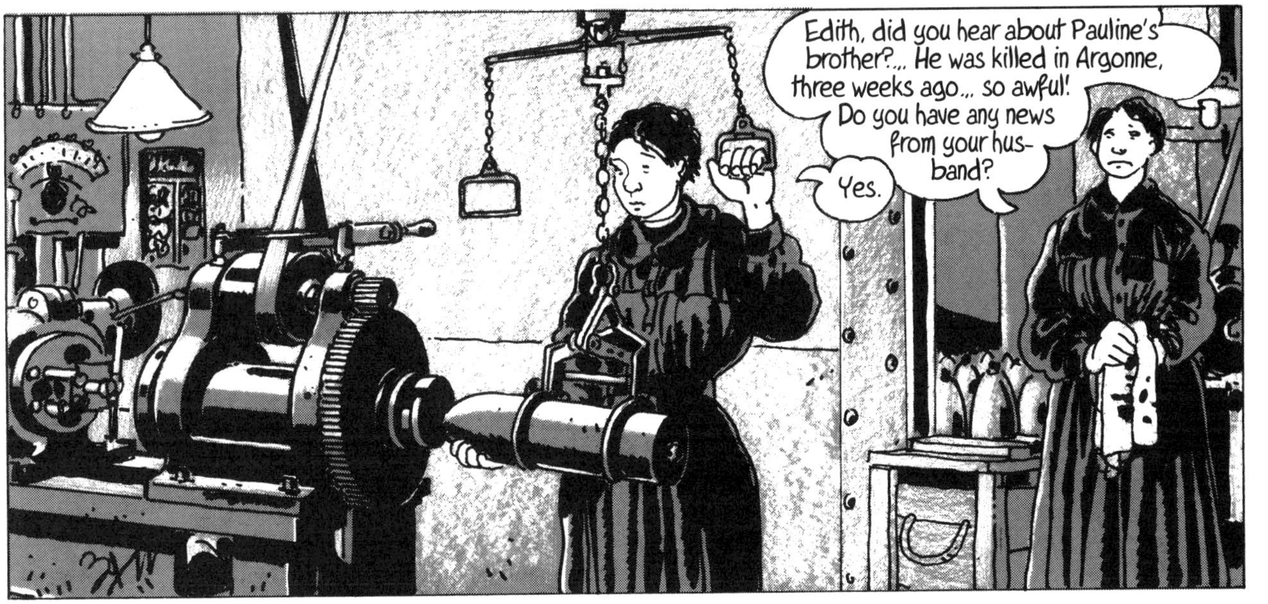
Edith, did you hear about Pauline's brother?... He was killed in Argonne, three weeks ago... so awful! Do you have any news from your husband?
Yes.

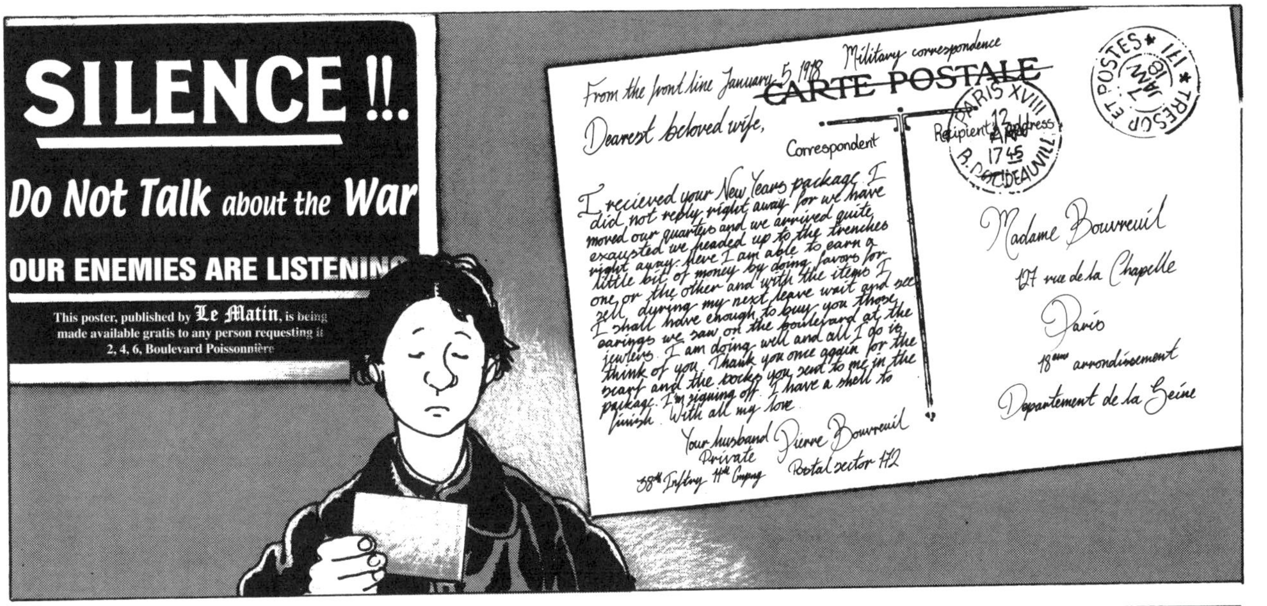
SILENCE !!.
Do Not Talk about the War
OUR ENEMIES ARE LISTENIN
This poster, published by Le Matin, is being made available gratis to any person requesting it 2, 4, 6, Boulevard Poissonnière
From the front line January 5 1918
Military correspondence
CARTE POSTALE
Dearest beloved wife,
Correspondent
Recipient's address
PARIS XVIII 12 17 45 R. DE DEAUVILL
POSTES ET TRESOR 171 17 JAN 18
I recieved your New Years package I did not reply right away for we have moved our quarters and we arrived quite exausted we headed up to the trenches right away. Here I am able to earn a little bit of money by doing favors for one or the other and with the items I sell during my next leave wait and see I shall have enough to buy you those earings we saw on the boulevard at the jewlers. I am doing well and all I do is think of you. Thank you once again for the scarf and the socks you sent to me in the package. I'm signing off. I have a shell to finish. With all my love
Your husband Pierre Bourreuil
Private
38th Infntry 11th Cmpny
Postal sector 172
Madame Bourreuil
127 rue de la Chapelle
Paris
18eme arrondissement
Departement de la Seine

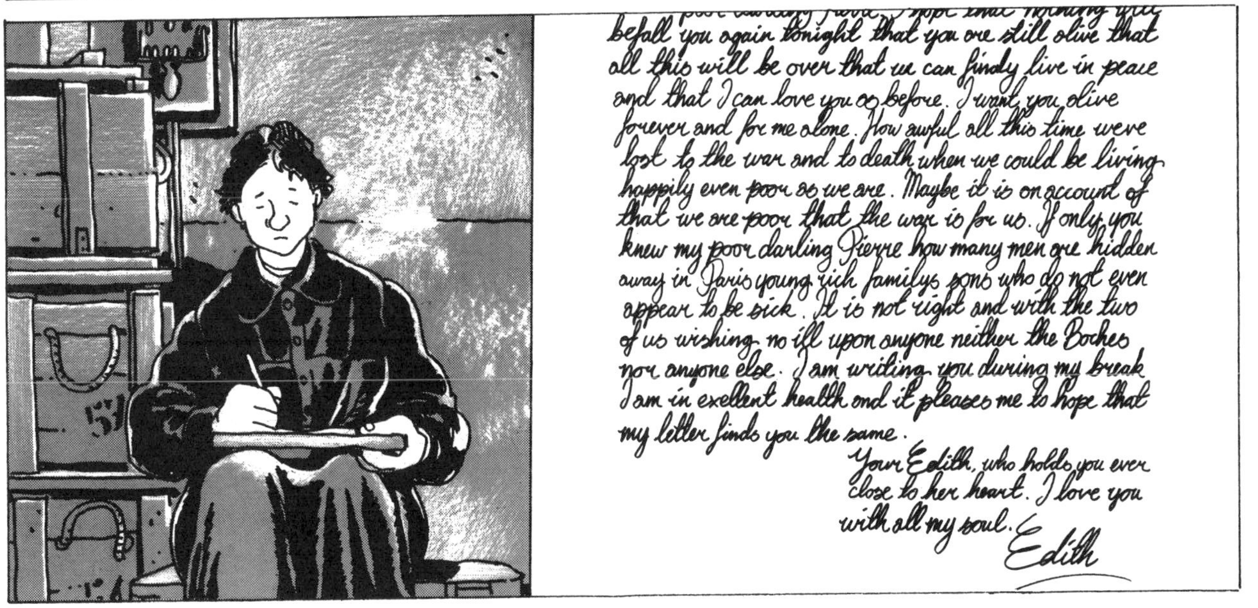
befall you again tonight that you are still alive that all this will be over that we can finaly live in peace and that I can love you as before. I want you alive forever and for me alone. How awful all this time we're lost to the war and to death when we could be living happily even poor as we are. Maybe it is on account of that we are poor that the war is for us. If only you knew my poor darling Pierre how many men are hidden away in Paris young rich familys sons who do not even appear to be sick. It is not right and with the two of us wishing no ill upon anyone neither the Boches nor anyone else. I am writing you during my break I am in exellent health and it pleases me to hope that my letter finds you the same.
Your Edith, who holds you ever close to her heart. I love you with all my soul.
Edith

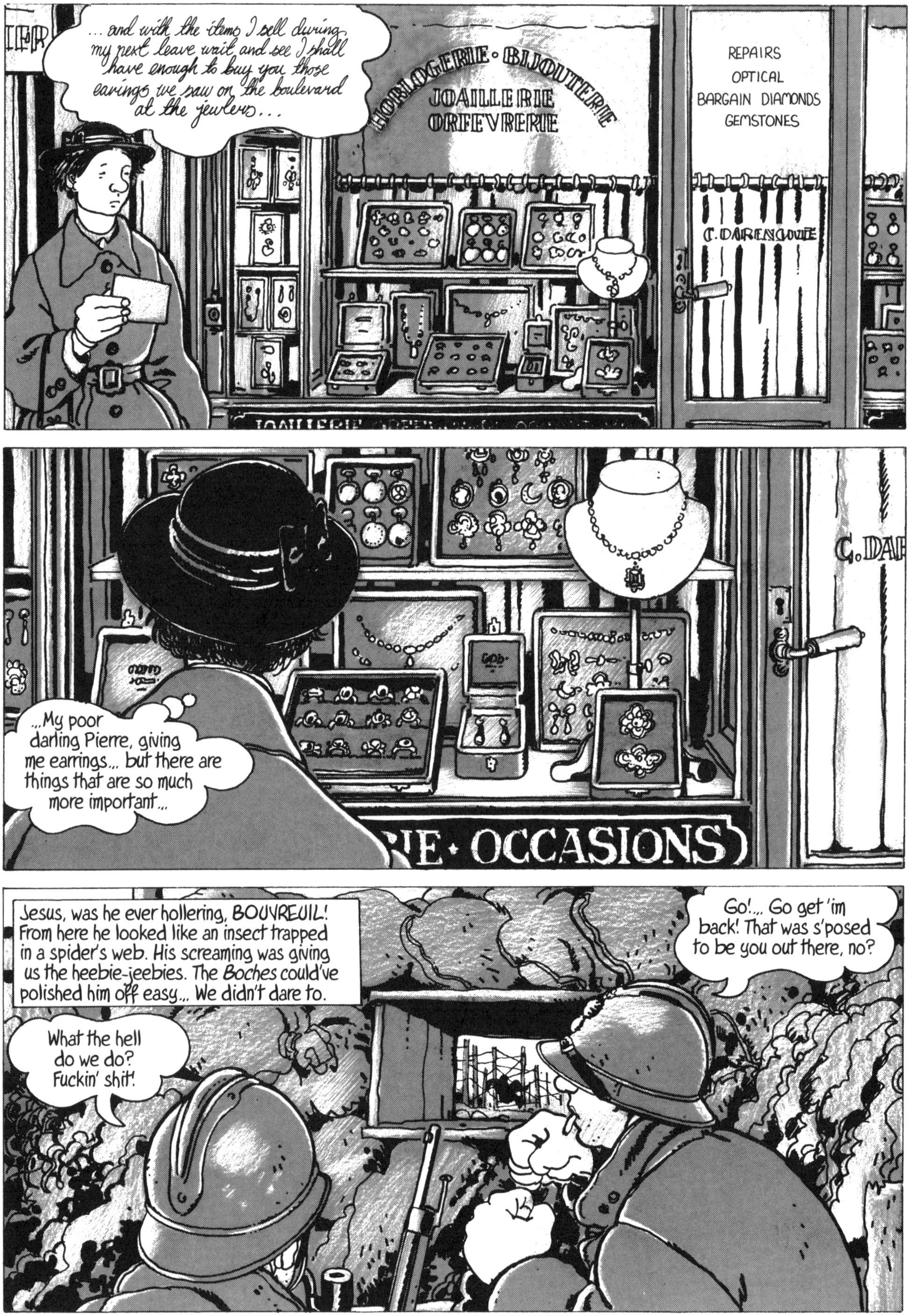
... and with the items I sell during my next leave wait and see I shall have enough to buy you those earings we saw on the boulevard at the jewlers...
HORLOGERIE • BIJOUTERIE
JOAILLERIE
ORFEVRERIE
REPAIRS
OPTICAL
BARGAIN DIAMONDS
GEMSTONES
...My poor darling Pierre, giving me earrings... but there are things that are so much more important...
RIE • OCCASIONS
Jesus, was he ever hollering, BOUVREUIL! From here he looked like an insect trapped in a spider's web. His screaming was giving us the heebie-jeebies. The *Boches* could've polished him off easy... We didn't dare to.
Go!... Go get 'im back! That was s'posed to be you out there, no?
What the hell do we do? Fuckin' shit!

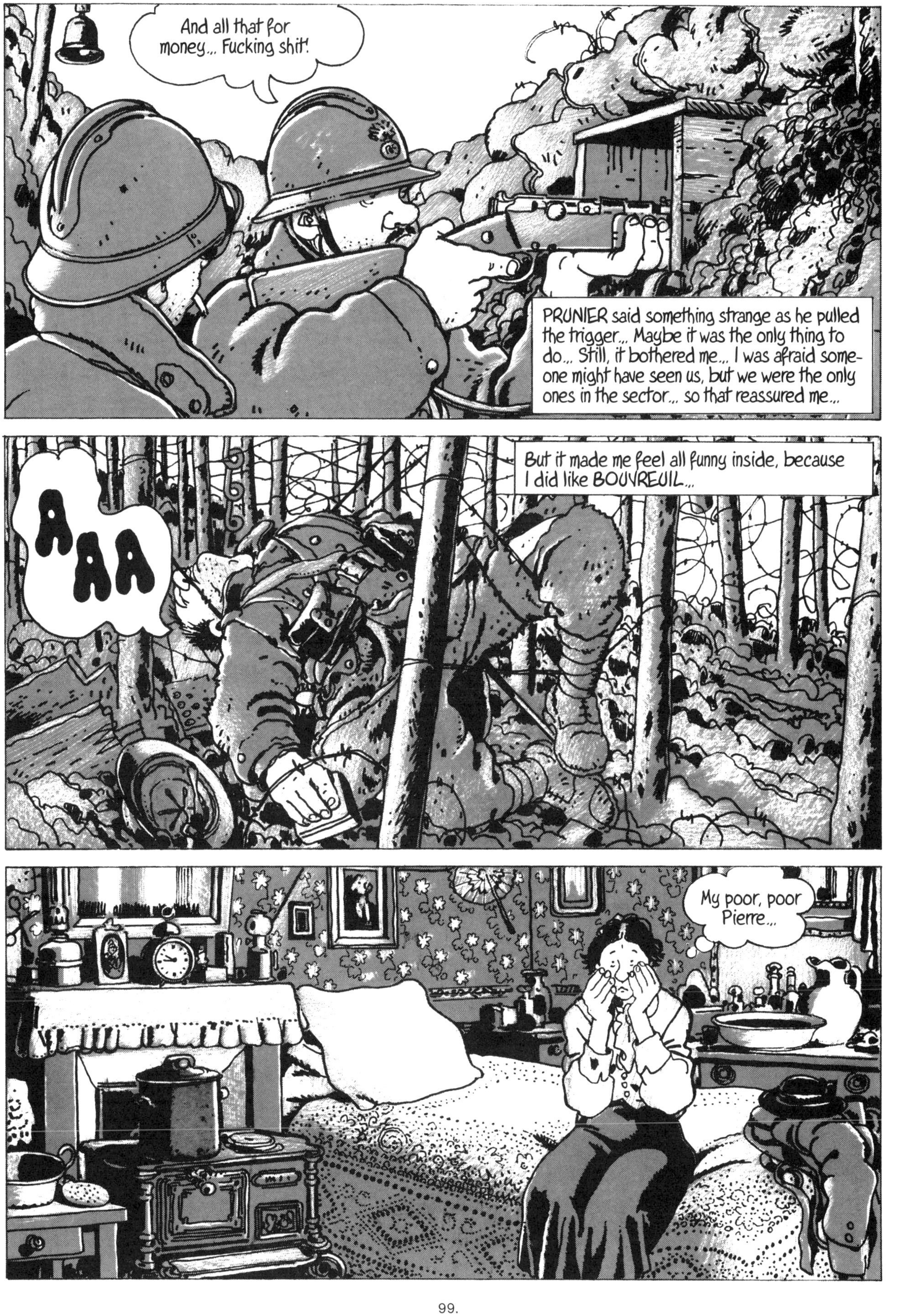
And all that for money... Fucking shit!
PRUNIER said something strange as he pulled the trigger... Maybe it was the only thing to do... Still, it bothered me... I was afraid someone might have seen us, but we were the only ones in the sector... so that reassured me...
But it made me feel all funny inside, because I did like BOUVREUIL...
AAA
My poor, poor Pierre...

As it turned out, no one got to go on leave that day...

GAS!!!

The alert was called, so we put on our equipment and waited.

There we were, sitting in the ditch like damn fools... No artillery to give us advance warning and suddenly, they were on top of us! They were in the trench before we even knew it.

Our cannons responded, but they were poorly adjusted and were hitting our lines. We quit messing around, we were forced to take off as best we could, to scramble from the trench to seek "refuge" between the lines.

Finally it stopped. We had no idea where our positions were any more. Disorientated *Boches* were returning from our side.,. I saw our Captain head into the German trench. We were staggering about, disgusted that we'd gone to all that trouble for nothing, because no one'd gained an inch of terrain.,.

I could hear PRUNIER screaming from my hole, and then I saw him make a grab for the "Muratti's after lunch" box, the artist's toolbox.,. with my eyes I saw it, the son of a bitch!

COME GET ME!.,. Don't leave me here!.,. I got money!.,. I got my leave on me... I'm off tonight to see my fiancée... Hurry! I can't miss the train leavin' for the rear! I ain't dead, don't leave me here!

Sometimes you had to bribe the stretcher-bearers.,. especially if your life wasn't worth much.

Me, I had a good wound, my pins all torn up, the war was over for me.,. Hospital, r 'n' r for a while, that was my immediate future.,. Life was beautiful. Night was falling, the stretcher jockeys were gonna be able to come and evacuate me.

When I saw the stretcher jockeys without their masks, I knew there was no risk any more, so I took off my rig...

...And I fucked up seriously by taking a deep breath! I hadn't realized the mustard gas'd collected at the bottom of the holes and caught myself a double lungful... Got some in my eyes, too... My very first gas attack.

103.

A giant communal grave, that's where they'd left us.

Corpses, corpses, everywhere... old ones, and ones that were still warm. There you had it in a nutshell! WORLD WAR ONE in all its "splendor"! 35 countries taking part, from near and far! What, you want numbers?... An "historical" accounting for the future? 10,000,000 dead! How many years of hope buried forevermore in the mud? How many orphaned? Maimed, widowed? In France alone, 2,300 acres of military cemeteries, fine soil for growing beets, but crosses are the only thing that grow there! If all the French war dead were to troop down the boulevard four abreast on Bastille Day, it would take at least six days and five nights for the last one to show his ashen face...

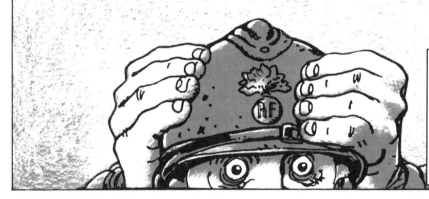

11 *départements*, 2,907 communes, 1,202,000 acres of forest, 4,760,000 acres of arable earth devastated! 794,040 houses and apartment buildings, 9,332 factories, 58,967 kilometers of roads, and 8,333 pieces of artwork destroyed, resulting in 71,000,000 cubic meters of trash!

You would need 330,000,000 cubic meters to fill up the 780 km of trenches on the front... and the cost? Cannons, shells, etc.? 2,500 billion Francs!

...For that price, every inhabitant of Europe — not to mention the Russians — could've been given a small four-room house... But, y'know, numbers!...

Setting up position in a cemetery wasn't such a hot idea...

But how'd we end up here? ... At this disaster, this shame, this rollback of all of civilization?

Now we had to regain the dressing station. And I wasn't even wounded, I was following in the steps of the maimed, just as I'd always followed the others... to my great misfortune.

Look at this one, giving the gawkers a laugh by forcing some poor bastard, maybe a farmer like himself, but German, to carry him....anyway...

And you, Englishman, you were sent as an ally and a neighbor, but I'm sure you're regretting it now.

AID STATION

Poor Sikh, your masters threw you into the carnage, and you think of your country.

Starting with the inhabitants of the United Kingdom and including the Canadians, Australians, New Zealanders, South Africans, and Indians, over 900,000 British subjects will die to protect the interests of the English crown... but not all of them fell with the frog-eaters.

Senegalese, your Gaulish forebears are proud of you. You're cold and you're dying for France. Absurd rumors about you abound, you're kept far from the white man's woman — the white man who exploits your lands and beats you. They will claim you were overjoyed at the idea of going to get your guts blown out, a grateful "big kid" happy to help the one who, for your own good, imposed his own religion, his hooch, and his TB.

Poor slave, poor beast of burden, it's death itself they make you carry on your shoulders!

...And it all ends here, in the dressing station.

And you, the Algerian who came from Atlas to die in Artois! Not that we'll be grateful! Why should we be — after all, you're French!!..., But that won't last. You and your son will battle the colonist who is growing vineyards on the lands he stole from you. You'll chase him out!

Shrieks of pain, stench of blood and excrement... we're back in the dressing station.

North African soldiers... 36,000 casualties... Your presence frightens even the veteran... When he sees you come up, he knows something serious is brewing, you may be first in line but he'll be next.

Vietnamese, you've seen the world thanks to the French! Endlessly exploitable as excavators, gravediggers...! Keep digging!

Forty years later, you'll be standing around a basin that'll serve as a communal burial ground for the French army, and which will include German legionnaires whom you will also kill as you liberate your country!

They've brought back two Germans — one is dying, but the other one is happy, the war is over for him.

He is interrogated, but what does he have to say? Other than that he wants to go home. As if this kid could know the secrets of the Kaiser's strategy? He has no information whatsoever, all he wants is to see his parents and his Hildegard again.

Cramped and undernourished, yes... but here the sky, though heavy with rain, is at least not heavy with deadly metal... so life is good. You get treated decently, because there are Frenchmen on the other side in the same situation... It's in between that it's hell.

A glass of crummy red for five pennies... you hope to die drunk, but fear sobers you up again...

You hear the monstrous rumbling in the distance, so you advance in silence.

We pause briefly for the impromptu execution of a villager. He was a spy, or so we'd heard...

The Russians leave. They don't want to fight any more. In la Courtine, in the middle of France where we'd quarantined them, they put up a banner: "DOWN WITH WAR." The Czar has just abdicated and they want to go home because of the Revolution.

...There were 16,000 in France and their officers can't control them any more... So we shot some of them, deported some of them... How many? Censored! They eventually get them evacuated.

Here come the Yanks... They hesitated for a long time before coming... The Vietnamese watch them go by with curiosity.

Ammunition for the cannons...

Cannon fodder.

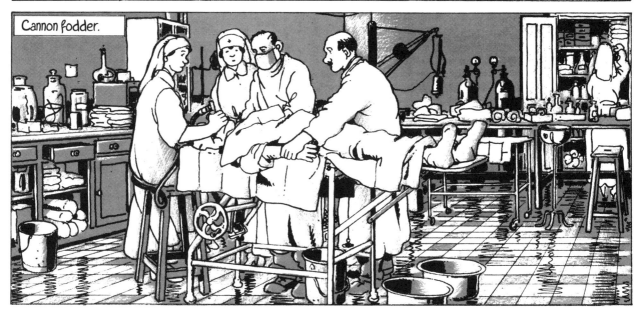

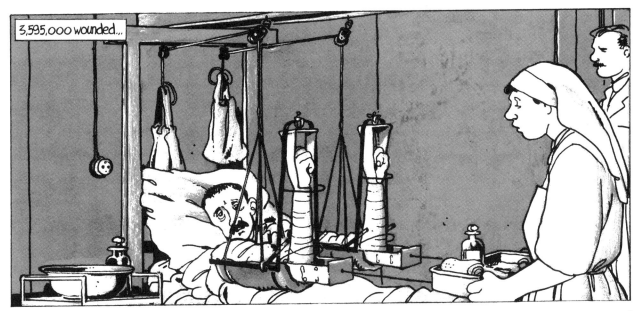

3,595,000 wounded...

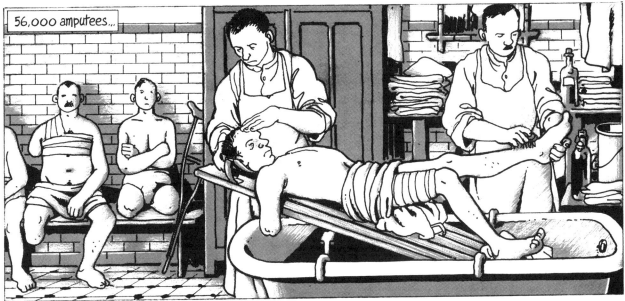

56,000 amputees...

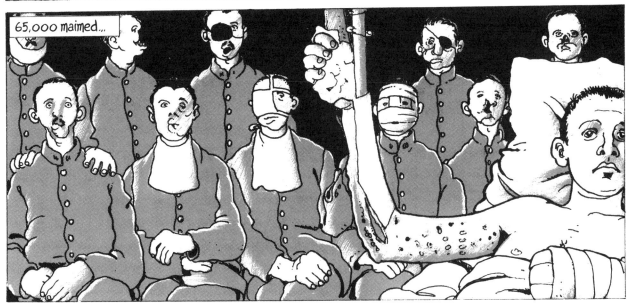

65,000 maimed...

The prisoners are walking on the parapet. They'll eventually get blown away
by stray bullets, but the sector will
be a little quieter while they pass...
I'm back. I got lost, I don't even know
where the hell I am now. In which trench,
and for how much longer, the mud, the
cold, the rats, the fear, and the lice?

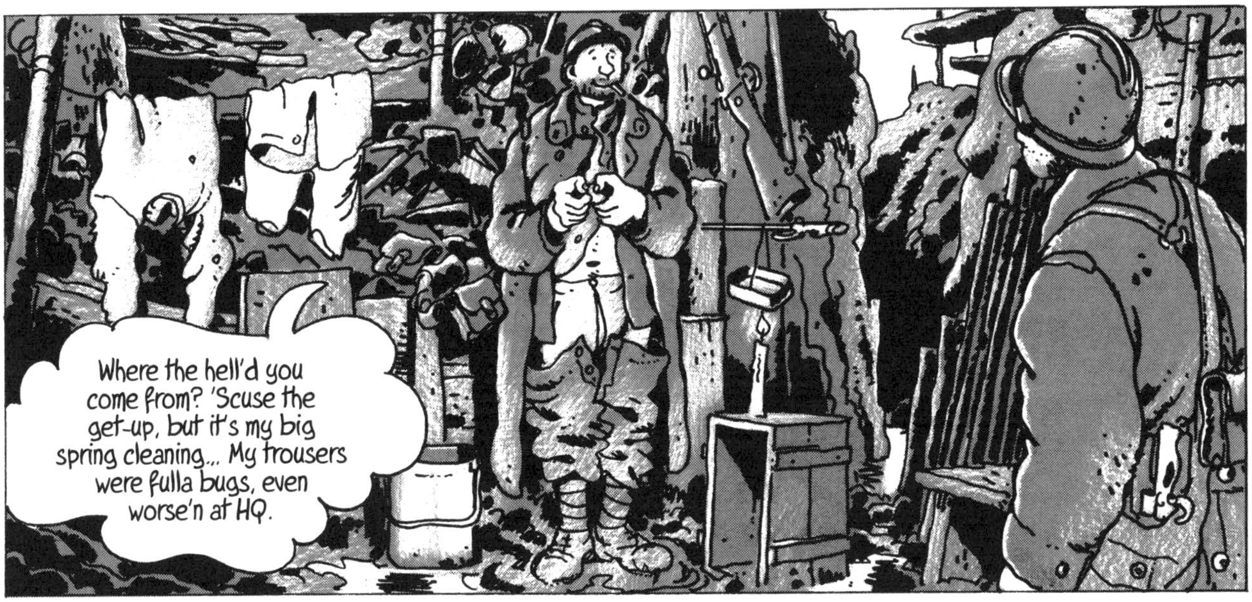
Where the hell'd you come from? 'Scuse the get-up, but it's my big spring cleaning... My trousers were fulla bugs, even worse'n at HQ.

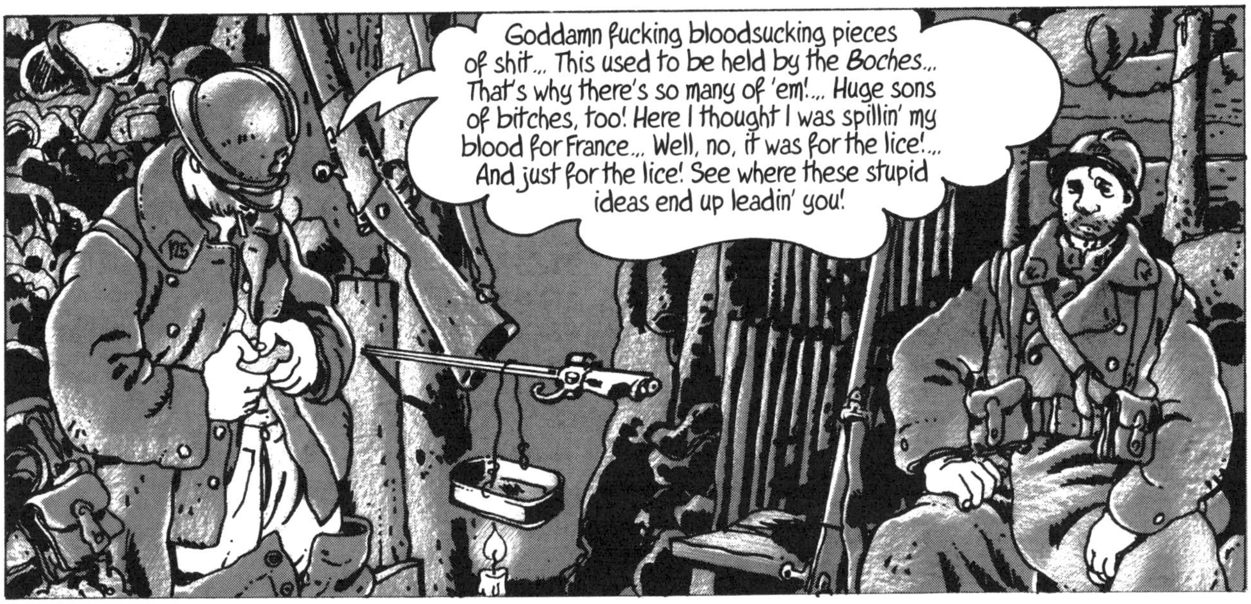
Goddamn fucking bloodsucking pieces of shit... This used to be held by the *Boches*... That's why there's so many of 'em!... Huge sons of bitches, too! Here I thought I was spillin' my blood for France... Well, no, it was for the lice!... And just for the lice! See where these stupid ideas end up leadin' you!

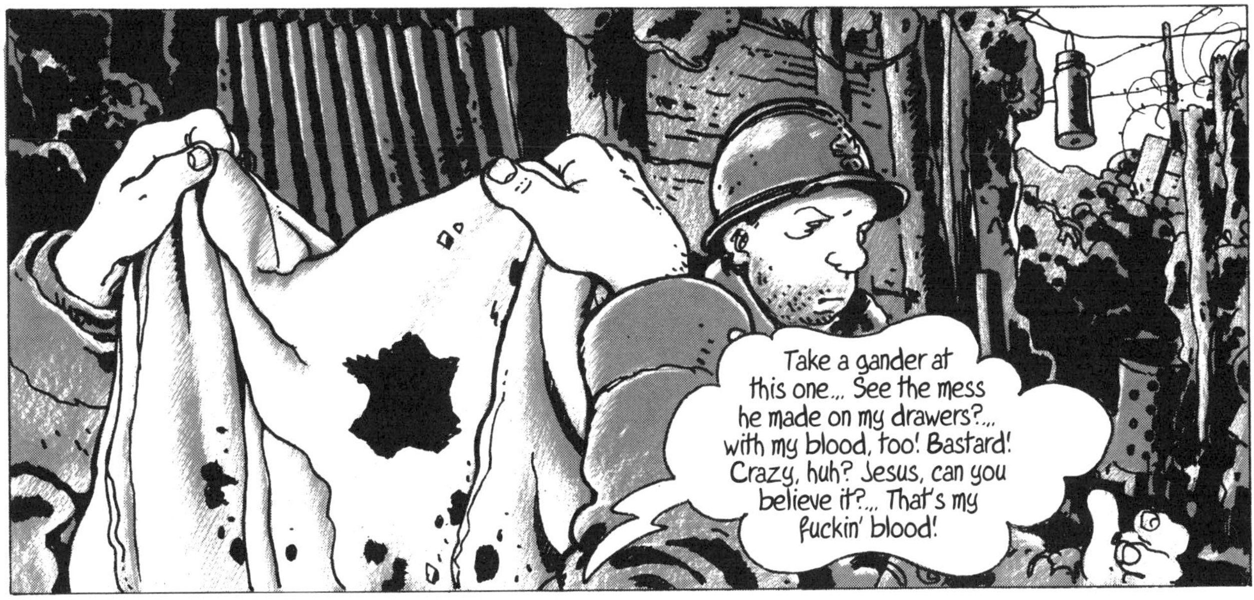
Take a gander at this one... See the mess he made on my drawers?... with my blood, too! Bastard! Crazy, huh? Jesus, can you believe it?... That's my fuckin' blood!

Setting up position in a cemetery wasn't such a hot idea... corpses... old ones, and ones that were still warm... Anyway, I killed my Bavarian like at a county fair, point blank. I saw him clearly. He was a kid. He was young enough to have acne, tiny gumdrops all over his cheeks. He had no business bein' here, he'd've been better off with his momma or with me at a bar. Hell, we even could've knocked back a few together... fraternized, in other words... But that ain't what happened and since they gave each of us a rifle, it was inevitable we'd end up murdering each other... and there you have it!

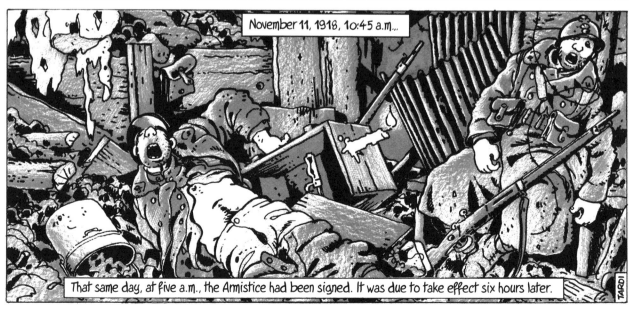

November 11, 1918, 10:45 a.m...

That same day, at five a.m., the Armistice had been signed. It was due to take effect six hours later.

118.

# FILMOGRAPHY

*J'accuse*, Abel Gance, 1918

*Shoulder Arms*, Charles Chaplin, 1918 †

*The Big Parade*, King Vidor, 1925 *

*Last Flight* (a.k.a. *The Crew*), Maurice Tourneur, 1928 *

*Verdun, Vision of History*, Léon Poirier, 1928 **

*The Dawn Patrol*, Howard Hawks, 1930 *

*All Quiet on the Western Front*, Lewis Milestone, 1930

*Westfront 1918*, George W. Pabst, 1930

*Wooden Crosses*, Raymond Bernard, 1931 †

*Broken Lullaby* (a.k.a. *The Man I Killed*), Ernst Lubitsch, 1932

*A Farewell to Arms*, Frank Borzage, 1932

*The Crew*, Anatole Litvak, 1935 *

*The Road to Glory*, Howard Hawks, 1936

*Grand Illusion*, Jean Renoir, 1937

*J'accuse* (2nd version) (a.k.a. *I Accuse That They May Live*),
Abel Gance, 1938

*Sergeant York*, Howard Hawks, 1941

*Devil in the Flesh*, Claude Atan Lara, 1946

*What Price Glory?*, John Ford, 1952

*A Farewell to Arms*, Charles Vidor, 1957

*Paths of Glory*, Stanley Kubrick, 1957

*Lafayette Escadrille* (a.k.a. *C'est la Guerre* or *With You in My
Arms*, U.K. *Hell Bent for Glory*), William Wellman, 1958

*The Great War*, Mario Monicelli, 1959

*King and Country*, Joseph Losey, 1964

*14-18*, Jean Aurel, 1964 *

*Thomas the Impostor*, Georges Franju, 1964 *

*The Blue Max*, John Guillermin, 1969

*Horizon*, Jacques Rouffio, 1967 *

*Oh! What a Lovely War*, Richard Attenborough, 1969

*Many Wars Ago*, Francesco Rosi, 1970 *

*Von Richthofen and Brown* (a.k.a. *The Red Baron*),
Roger Corman, 1971

*Johnny Got His Gun*, Dalton Trumbo, 1971

*Fort Saganne*, Alain Corneau, 1983 **

*Life and Nothing But*, Bertrand Tavernier, 1989

*Angel's Wing*, Richard Dembo, 1992

* not released on DVD (the *Dawn Patrol* available on DVD is the
non-Hawks 1938 remake starring Errol Flynn and Basil Rathbone;
*The Big Parade* was released in a now out-of-print VHS version)

** not released on U.S. format DVD

† *Wooden Crosses* available in a box set with *Les Misérables*;
*Shoulder Arms* available in various Chaplin collections.

# BIBLIOGRAPHY

*Under Fire*, Henri Barbusse, 1916

*The Bomb-Shell*, Maurice Leblanc, 1916

*Ceux de 14 (Men of '14)*, Maurice Genevoix (4 volumes), 1916-1921 *

*The New Book of Martyrs*, Georges Duhamel, 1917

*Wooden Crosses*, Roland Dorgelès, 1919

*Storm of Steel*, Ernst Jünger, 1920

*The Devil in the Flesh*, Joseph Kessel, 1923

*Thomas the Impostor*, Jean Cocteau, 1923

*All Quiet on the Western Front*, Erich Maria Remarque, 1928

*Death of a Hero*, Richard Aldington, 1929

*Four Infantrymen on the Western Front*, Ernst Johannsen, 1929

*Témoins (Witnesses)*, Jean Norton Cru, 1929 *

*Return of the Brute*, Liam O'Flaherty, 1930

*The Road Back*, Erich Maria Remarque, 1931

*To the Slaughterhouse*, Jean Giono, 1931

*A Farewell to Arms*, Ernest Hemingway, 1932

*Les Hommes de bonne volonté (Men of Good Will)*, 20 volumes,
    Jules Romains, 1932-1947 *

*Captain Conan*, Roger Vercel, 1934

*Fear*, Gabriel Chevallier, 1934

*Verdun*, Jacques Pericard, 1934 *

*Paths of Glory*, Humphrey Cobb, 1935

*Refus d'Obéissance (Refusal to Obey)*, Jean Giono, 1936 *

*Johnny Got His Gun*, Dalton Trumbo, 1939

*The Severed Hand*, Blaise Cendrars, 1946

*1914-1918, vie et mort des Français (1914-1918, Life and Death of the
    French)*, André Ducasse, Jacques Meyer, Gabriel Perrieux, 1962 *

*The Mutineries of 1917 (The 1917 Mutinies)*, Guy Pedroncini, 1967

*La Mort de près (Death Close Up)*, Maurice Genevoix, 1972

*Le Temps des Américains, 1917-1918 (The Time of the Americans,
    1917-1918)*, André Kaspi, 1976 *

*Adieu la vie, adieu l'amour (Goodbye Life, Goodbye Love)*, Amand
    Lanoux, 1977

*Les Carnets de guerre de Louis Barthas, tonnelier (The War Diaries of
    Louis Barthas, Barrel Maker)*, 1978 *

*Les pelotons du general Pétain (General Pétain's Squads)* Vincent Moulia,
    1978

*The Great War and the French People*, Jean-Jacques Becker, 1980

*Le Pantalon (The Pants)*, Alain Scoff *

*La Femme au temps de la guerre de 14 (Women at the Time of the
    1914 War)*, Francoise Thébaud, 1986 *

*A Very Long Engagement*, Sébastien Japrisot, 1991

*Clavel Soldat (Private Clavel)*, Léon Werth, 1993 *

*Les Fusillés*, Blanche Maupas, 1994 *

*Carnets d'un Survivant (A Survivor's Notebooks)*, Dominique Richert, 1994 *

* indicates works not released in English; titles translations by K.T.

## ABOUT THE ARTIST

Jacques Tardi, who has just entered his fifth decade as one of the defining cartoonists of his generation, was born in Valence, France in 1946. Tardi broke into *Pilote* magazine with a series of short stories beginning in 1969, soon graduating to graphic novels. In 1976, he launched (for Editions Casterman) his turn-of-the-century serial *Adèle Blanc-Sec*, of which nine volumes have appeared, most recently (after a decade-long hiatus) *Le Labyrinthe Infernal* in 2007. The unsmiling heroine is being adapted into a trilogy of movies ("Indiana Jones meets Amélie") by director/producer Luc Besson, with the first installment slated for release in 2010.

Tardi's more than 30 graphic novels to date include a number of books about World War I (most recently the two-volume *Putain de Guerre*) and a long run of detective and crime thrillers, of which five star Léo Malet's Paris-based private eye Nestor Burma. Tardi was the Grand Prize winner of the 1985 Angoulême comics convention.

Tardi continues to produce graphic novels at a pace that would be daunting to car-toonists half his age. His next release, after the just-completed concluding volume of *Putain de Guerre*, will be his third book based on a story by Jean-Patrick Manchette (after the col-laboration *Griffu* and the adaptation *West Coast Blues*), *La Position du tireur couché* (*The Prone Gunman.*)

## ABOUT THIS BOOK

As Jacques Tardi notes in his introduction, The Great War – that gaping wound in Europe's history from which has sprung seemingly every horror that has afflicted us since – was on his mind from the beginning. As a child, he was haunted by his grandfather's war stories; the War was the subject of the first "real" book he read; and when he tried, at the tender age of 22, to sell his first professional comics story to *Pilote* magazine, that was the subject he chose. (It was rejected.)

While Tardi's work has ranged through many genres and many periods, from the 1812 war through modern-day France to a faux-Roman post-apocalyptic future, he returns to that conflict again and again, sometimes glancingly (as in the *Adele Blanc-Sec* series, whose heroine sleeps through it, although she wakes up to witness its ghastly residue), sometimes head-on – as he does here (and his most recent work, *Putain de guerre!*).

*It Was the War of the Trenches* endured the longest gestation period of any Tardi book: Launched in 1982 in the pages of the legendary French comics anthology *(A SUIVRE)* and then continued two years later in the hardcover *Le trou d'obus* (pp. 9-28 of the present edition), it was abandoned for close to a decade and finally completed, once again in *(A SUIVRE)*, in 1993.

But if French readers suffered a patience-straining 12-year wait between publication of the first and final episodes, *Trenches'* long march to English-language publication doubled that: *RAW* Magazine published an early chapter in 1983 (pp. 31-38); then Drawn and Quarterly cherry-picked three of the latter chapters for its flagship anthology over a decade later. It appears here complete in English for the first time, and newly translated, too – except for the *RAW* segment whose translator, Kim Thompson, vowed 26 years ago that he would some day complete the job. And so he has.